Barrio Side Hero

Enrique S. Flores

Floricanto Press

Copyright © 2019 by Enrique S. Flores

Copyright © 2019 of this edition by Floricanto and Berkeley Presses

All rights reserved. No part of this publication may be stored in a retrieval system, transmitted or reproduced in any way, including but not limited to photocopy, photograph, magnetic, laser or other type of record, without prior agreement and written permission of the publisher.

Floricanto is a trademark of Floricanto Press.

Berkeley Press is an imprint of Inter-American Development, Inc.

Floricanto Press
7177 Walnut Canyon Rd.
Moorpark, California 93021
415 793-2662

www.FloricantoPress.com

ISBN-13 9781795159043

"Por nuestra cultura hablarán nuestros libros. Our books shall speak for our culture."

Roberto Cabello-Argandoña and Leyla Namazie, Editors

Dedicated to,
My East Side Heroes' Family.

Dedicated to,
All those currently aboard their double-duce journey .

OLD SOUL

THUMB-thum, THUMB-thum, THUMB-thum! My heart pounded as I sprinted my hardest across the desolate desert. Suddenly, I heard a deafening sound three miles behind me, KABOOM! I looked back and saw a tall broccoli-shaped cloud of smoke rising from the missile's impact site.

I sprinted even faster now. Why? Because I knew exactly what was coming next. In less than twenty seconds, I ran and dashed behind large boulders, just as a heavy wall of sand blew past me from all around me. After the brief sand storm ended, I continued to sit there, catching my breath in relief. With my back against the stone, my heart rate began to slow down.

Faintly, I heard voices in the far distance - voices of a dozen or so enemy soldiers fast approaching, as they searched for me. I got up to my feet, kept my upper body bent low, and scurried quietly between larger boulders. I hid behind a bigger stone, and I held my breath, trying to make myself invisible. My heart rate began pounding fast again, THUMB-thum, THUMB-thum, THUMB-thum! - As I realized I had no-where to hide, no-where to run. I was now outnumbered, out-gunned, and out of time. I heard the enemy soldiers, climbing over the rocks, from all directions as they barked orders to each other to check well behind each rock. As I heard their voices getting closer, surrounding me, an ice-cold wave of terror splashed over my entire body, causing me to hyperventilate and gasp for air with shallow and rapid short breaths as I suffered a paralyzing panic-attack, at the worst possible moment.

As they closed in, they discovered my hiding place! One of the hate-filled soldiers climbed over a massive boulder above me, and without mercy, without hesitation, within two quick seconds, he aims his rifle at me and opens fire. All goes black. Next, without my material body, I then feel myself flying through a black space or tunnel, expanding and shrinking every few seconds. I expand as big and cushiony as the gigantic "marsh-mellow-man," feeling light-headed.

I re-lived this same "dream" every day, over and over, along with all of its vivid details, multiple times each day, for six consecutive weeks. My parents tell me that those six weeks were the longest weeks during my infancy, because I was severely ill, with a persistent fever of 103 degrees that would not go away nor decrease. My parents tell me I was so physically weak, I hardly ate, did not respond to sounds, and I hardly cried at all during those six weeks. My mom had to stop working to tend to her sick child. The medicine that the doctors prescribed did not help. Feeling desperate to find a cure, my mom applied an old home-remedy she learned from her mom back in Mexico, and miraculously, the fever finally broke, and in less than twenty-four hours I was better. Later on, I asked my parents how old I was when I got sick? My mom stated, *"Tenías apenas nueve meses de nacido, m'ijo."*

PROLOGUE

CROSS ROADS

I will fear no evil, for you are with me...
Surely your goodness and love will follow me
all the days of my life..." —Psalm 23.

Standing in the middle of my "Story and King" cross-roads, like Tom Hanks in the movie, "Cast Away", I look at each road ahead of me and wait in silence. I stand there gazing at each of the four roads enticing me. Trying to visualize the result of each. I stand there in silence - listening to the breeze, hoping for a deliberate sign. Nothing. Growing impatient, I reach inside myself to retrieve my answer.

The road ahead of me is named, LOGIC. It is the obvious choice, because the positives outweigh the negatives. This road tells me, "Don't be stupid. Do you want to be broke for ever?! What are you waiting? Hurry up! You're wasting time!" When traveling on this road, I apply for jobs that pay the most money.

The road to my left side is named, EMOTION. This road tells me, "Look! This road feels new, exciting, fun, safe, and easy - you won't feel stressed about anything. You deserve this rest. Why are you working so hard?" When I am traveling on this road, I quit jobs or friendships that cause me any feelings of anxiety.

The road behind is named, TRAUMA. This road constantly reminds me, "Don't forget all your past failures. Everybody remembers how embarrassing your defeats were. Never forget or it will happen again and it WILL be all your fault. This road reminds me, 'Trust No One' and 'Prepare for the End'." This road haunts me with questions of shame that repeats over and over again, such as, "Do you think you will get away with that? How come you abandoned that person and haven't reached out to them? When are you coming back to fix this? Are you just going to pretend it never happened? Just watch, when everybody finds out your dirty little secrets, what then? You haven't changed at all, you are who you are, you'll never change; "If you put perfume on shit, it's still shit."

When I am on this road, called TRAUMA. I want to search for my ex's; I want to hang out with old friends and remember the old times; I want to return to old jobs; and I want to recall all those whom have harmed me and seek revenge "Round 2".

But, then, a gentle breeze nudges me from the right side… This road is named, INTUITION. This road never says much. This path is always mute. Or maybe I never tried listening? Maybe because the other three paths are so much louder, persistent, insistent, and demanding. This road, INTUITION whispers. INTUITION whispers tiny "hints," one or two words at a time. This road INTUITION uses other people to indirectly communicate a message. Sometimes it shows me a movie clip in my dreams. Sometimes it hides its' messages in the Metro Horoscope. Sometimes, it disguises itself amongst my other random thoughts.

But if I tune-in to the right station, like when I read Paulo Coelho's books, "The Alchemist," "The Warrior of Light," INTUITION talks to me directly in every page. On rare occasions, I can understand why INTUITION allows shitty situations to occur in my life, and then asks me, "And? What are you going to do about it? What is your soul ? Who or what do you trust?

But, with all the other three roads trying to get my attention, I stand there, at the cross-roads, in discernment, waiting for multiple signs to confirm the direction; waiting for the messengers; waiting for clarity of vision; waiting for a calling; waiting for divine inspiration.

Sometimes, I wait too long. Sometimes, I give into LOGIC, EMOTION, and TRAUMA. Then, to cope, I eat junk food to "comfort me," I stay "busy" with work, and I worry to stay distracted from feeling my emotions. And when I lift my eyes again to look at the cross-roads again. I feel lost and exhausted. I don't trust my brain anymore. I don't trust the steps I take. I feel like giving up, doing nothing, sleeping all the time.

"The Past Lives in our Memory;
The Future Lives in our Imagination;
The Present Lives in Feeling our Emotions."

I'VE GOT ISSUES,

"Depression = is Suppression"

I feel like I'm one of those characters in the TV show, "LOST." I feel like I'm wandering in my Purgatory - stuck in Limbo. I need to heal whatever went wrong back then. So that only goodness will exists in me. And then, and only then will I be made whole again, restored to my original worth.

Great Mentor, "…grant me the Serenity
To accept the things I can not change,
Courage to change the things I can;
And the wisdom to know the difference." - Reinhold Niebuhr

"All Anxiety - is Avoidance," my therapist told me. Then I ask myself, "What am I avoiding?" What makes things worse is that because I've stayed emotionally numb for so long, I hardly have any memories at all. I've avoided "feeling." Even my depression is avoidance, because depression is a suppression of emotions. I am avoiding feeling my feelings. But why? Why am I avoiding? What came BEFORE my depression? Well, before my depression I stayed busy with my General Anxiety Disorder. And, before my General Anxiety, I stayed busy with my work-a-holism. And, before being a work-a-holic, I was a sex-a-holic for six years. And, before my sex addiction I was busy being in hate-mode for about four years, starving for revenge on all my past enemies. And what came before the hate? Well, before the hate, I was constantly paranoid for about two years, due to my Post-Traumatic Stress Disorder. And before my paranoia I was in constant flight mode, for about five years non-stop, because in those few years, avoiding death and incarceration was a full time job. And before the paranoia I experienced a low-self esteem because school kids ridiculed my clothes, looks, and speech. And before being ridiculed, I felt desperate panic and fear because my mom suffered from frequent fainting spells, at random times, she would collapse to the floor and stop breathing. And I would run to her, lift her head, tap her on the cheek many times and plead with her to breathe, "Mom! Mom! Breathe!" And one of us would run to get the rubbing alcohol, and once we put some under her nostrils, she would wake up to the intense smell. And before that desperation, I felt loss of protection, realizing in third grade that protection from danger is not guaranteed, so I began to worry.

Before worry entered my spirit, before third grade, I used to love playing sports like soccer without worrying about being "good enough," I used to love to draw without fear of judgment; I used to love to laugh without being self-conscious of my crooked teeth; I used to feel safe. My therapist Dr. Harold Hoyle helped me realize all of this. I finally accepted the fact that I left my original-self back then, "chained to the tether-pole" in the third grade, eight years old. Once I realized this, I was excited to "go back" to find myself. BUT, as my therapist Dr. Hoyle said, "The answers are NOT 'out there'. They have always been 'within you'."

"He who can't cry, can't laugh either."
'The most important quality on the spiritual path is courage,' said Ghandi. The world seems threatening and dangerous to cowards. They seek the false security of a life with no major challenges and arm themselves to the teeth to defend what they think they possess. Cowards end up making the bars of their prison...These are the commandments that no warrior of light can obey,

First, God is sacrifice. Suffer in this life and you will be happy in the next.

Second, People who have fun are childish. Remain tense at all times.

Third, Other people know what is best for us because they have more experience.

Fourth, We must make other people happy. We must please them even if that means making major sacrifices.

Fifth, We must not drink from the cup of happiness; we might get to like it and won't always have it in our hands.

Sixth, We must accept all punishments. We are guilty.

Seventh, Fear is a warning. We don't want to take any risks." —Paulo Coelho *Warriors of Light*

So, I'll start from the beginning; because, we all start—where our parents left off.

CHAPTER I

DILEMMA

One morning, *mi Abuelito* said to his eldest son, my dad, "M'ijo, you have a choice to make, First, you can either go to *el norte,* the United States, and work to send money back to help our family; or, second, you can continue your studies here at *la secundaria,* High School... however, if you decide on school, I cannot afford to pay the tuition."

Faced with that choice, my dad arrived in Los Angeles, California a few months later. At age fifteen, his first job was working as a dishwasher. As the eldest son, it was his duty to help feed his nine younger siblings and obey his dad. As a fifteen-year-old teenager, my father was not ready to leave his friends, he did not want to leave his house, he did not want to leave his home-country, he did not want to move away from all his family and kin, nor he did not want to stop being a kid. My dad loved his hometown aka, *pueblito*. As a boy, he enjoyed hanging out inside the church, as a *monaguillo,* helping the priest prepare for mass.

But, at age fifteen, my dad was now "old enough" to face the world alone as "a man." As a "teenage man," he traveled alone across his country of Mexico, aboard *el camión.* This teenage man needed to defend himself against older men who tried to rob him. At age fifteen, my dad had only a few days to figure out how to survive in a new land, in a new country, with a new language, with new enforced laws, perform jobs he had never done before, and try to make new friends within a sea of strangers. But as many *paisanos* state, *No hay de otra.* There's no other option.

That same year, in a Mexican city called Durango, my mom at that time, age sixteen lived with her dad, her mom, and her three siblings. As daddy's girl, my grandfather would always say goodbye to his daughter, my mom, with a fatherly kiss on her forehead before he left for work each morning.

As in many families, things happen, and my mom's father became disappointed in her. So, he stopped saying goodbye to her in the mornings, stubbornly holding a grudge and rejecting her efforts to apologize. My mom woke up early every morning hoping her dad would finally forgive her and say goodbye in the mornings like he always used to. But he was a stubborn, traditional Mexican man with rigid expectations and refused to forgive. This is where my mom's depression began to take root. One morning, my mom saw her dad get ready for work in the morning, and once again—her dad ignored her and left without saying goodbye. That was the last moment my mom saw her dad alive. My grandpa never came back home. My mom's daddy died in a work accident.

Her safety, her rock, the only man of the house—was now gone. For the 1st time, her family experienced panic. Who's going to work? Who's going to bring in money to eat? Without any preparation, my grandmother became a widow and a single mom of four kids, all under seventeen years old. They struggled for a year - trying to survive, relying on the kindness of relatives and neighbors. Soon they realized that they had no other choice—"somebody" had to go to *El Norte*, the United States, and find a job that pays well. My mom packed a single suitcase and at age eighteen, she crossed *la línea* and found a job, in San Jose, California as a babysitter for an Asian family, taking care of two children. My mom sent the majority of her small paycheck back home to support her three siblings, along with a new-born infant, and her mom who suffers from chronic health issues and needed daily medication.

A few years later, my dad decided to move to northern California from LA to San Jose searching for better paying restaurant jobs. One spring morning, while my mom played volleyball with her friends at Kelly Park, aka "Happy Hollow," she saw my dad for the first time gazing at her. They began dating and soon my mom became pregnant. My dad decided to take my mom to meet his family in Mexico. While in Mexico, my mom pressured my dad to return to the United States soon. Her reason was simple yet profound. She told my dad, "My baby MUST be born in United States. He deserves more than I can give him." Thanks to my mom's insistence, both my brother and I were born as US citizens.

"Give me your tired, your poor,
Your huddled masses yearning to breathe free...
Send these, the homeless...
I lift my lamp beside the golden door." —Statue of Liberty

LA MIGRA'S MOST WANTED

One evening, my dad and my brother at that time, age five drove to "Lee's Burgers" to buy our family a greasy but delicious dinner. During those years, we lived across the street from Pink Elephant, in the apartments, on Virginia St. As my dad got into his car to turn on the engine, two INS Immigration ICE Agents immediately spotted my dad's brown skin. The ICE agents approached the driver side and in the presence of his five year old son, these uniformed men handcuff dad's wrists to the steering wheel. My dad pleaded with the two men in Spanish not take him away. My dad tried to explain to them that his son was a U.S.-born citizen and that he had another U.S.-born child and wife who depended on him financially, waiting for him at home. Miraculously, "La Migra" uncuffed my father—however, only under one strict condition —La Migra told my dad that he had to go home, pack up all their belongings and leave for Mexico with his family. They sternly explained that they would mail documents to his home address in Mexico, for my father to sign, mail back, to verify that he had returned to Mexico. My dad did as he was told. My mother and father packed whatever they could fit into our small family car and drove to Mexico.

During the three-day long drive to Mexico, my family stopped by my mom's hometown, to visit my mom's side of the family. It was in that city of Durango where I tasted my very first taco "con chile," at age two. I've been hooked on salsa ever since! Within a week of arriving at my dad's hometown, my dad and mom immediately began planning our return back to San Jose.

My mom and dad boarded a bus towards the border, carrying their two baby boys my brother age five, and myself, age two. Days later, the Flores Family arrived at the Mexico-US border. Everybody knew it was a dangerous crossing. There were few options for families like mine. We could either take our chances of dying of thirst in the hot desert. The sad facts are the Border Patrol find at least 366 bodies of men, women, and children who die each year from heat stroke and dehydration. We could choose to run all night through the dark mountains where wild animals and armed-robbers lay in wait. Or my family could hold-on-tight to each other's hands and run across the six-lane freeway trying to dodge hundreds of zooming cars speeding by. Or, finally, my family could instead risk drowning inside the Rio Bravo—like in the movie, "Mi Familia." My mom and dad stood in fright along side El Rio Grande's edge. They were worried about their sons' making it.

An elderly woman standing nearby saw my parents' dilemma and offered to cross my brother and I, legally *por la línea*—given the fact that my brother and I are U.S. citizens. Similar to the movie, "Under the Same Moon," this coyote-lady, aka "pollera," explained to my father that she could cross us boys, by utilizing one of her internal contacts at the border patrol. My dad, however, sternly and firmly stated five words that ended that conversation, *"Pasamos todos o nadie pasa."* We all cross, or nobody crosses.

My parents decided to boldly face the strongest natural element on earth - water. As they stood at the water's edge, my parents blessed each other and their children with the sign of the cross on their foreheads and chest, as two coyote-men stood-by ready to assist our family reach our new destiny. The first gentleman-coyote helped my mom cross the dangerous waters, the second coyote carried my brother age 5 across, making sure his head was always above the water's surface; and lastly, my dad sat me down on top of his shoulders, with my little feet wrapped around his neck.

Although I was only two years old, I remember very well the panic and shock my little body felt when we entered the freezing waters. I immediately began to cry hysterically as we entered into the deep frigid. All of my senses permanently memorized this traumatic experience. I clearly remember the up and down motion of my dad hopping on his tippy-toes across the river, trying to avoid stepping into holes or slipping on the rocks - all while trying to keep his nostrils above the water's surface. I began to cry even louder, terrified, because I thought we were going to dip under, and I didn't know how to swim. Maybe this is why I still have a phobia of swimming in the deep-end.

As we waded across the Rio Grande, my dad tried his best to reassure me that I was safe by saying, "Shhhh, shhh, shhh." He managed to quiet me down and avoiding detection. I'll never forget the feeling of the ice water splashing my two small legs and lower back, as my dad and I bounced in and out of the water's surface. My dad said he remembered seeing and hearing some French-sounding Reporters standing along the river's edge filming us and taking pictures. It's surreal to think that somewhere out there, there is actual footage and photographs - that on this cool evening, at dusk, I was officially baptized as a *"Mojado."*

"¡Aquí estamos, y no nos vamos! Y si nos llevan, regresamos!" —Grito Serpentino

FIRST EDUCATIONAL EXPERIENCE?

"What is your First Education Memory?" I was asked during a retreat. Good question I thought—I've never been asked that before. My first reaction was to go back to second grade, when an Asian boy pulled out a pocket knife about eight inches away from my belly. But, was that my **first** education experience? I tried to think back further; and a memory emerged of my first grade teacher getting so frustrated with a skinny ADHD white kid named Ryan. She forcefully pulled him back by his shirt, to the point where he flew backwards off of his chair, and then this Caucasian teacher dragged Ryan accross the floor by his hair all the way outside the class door, as Ryan yelled, "Ow!, Ow!, Ow!."

But was that **truly** my very "Fisrt Educational Experience?" Unsure, I challenged my memory even further and thought back before entering kindergarten - to my preschool year at Mayfair. I reached far back into the darkest corners of my memory bank, to retrieve an experience I had not remembered in over twenty years. I was four years old, attending Mayfair Preschool, when during recess a bully punched me hard on my chest. I walked away, with my head down, feeling sad and confused—not understanding why somebody would want to hurt me? Standing outside the main building, one of the teachers saw the assault and pointed at the bully, yelling the command "come here!" She then also pointed at me and gestured with her hands for me to go over as well.

Both of us kids stood there, in front of her, looking at the floor, in silence and in suspense. She seemed angry. She then told the bully, "Tell him you're sorry!" The boy, with no remorse in his voice, softly said, "Sorry." With my eyes still fixed downward, I nodded my head as to communicate, "It's ok. It's no big deal" attitude. But I couldn't believe my ears of what I heard next.

This preschool teacher turned to look at me and in a stern tone of voice, stated the order, "Now hit him back." My eyes opened wide as I looked at her in disbelief. With a perplexed expression on my face, I looked at the boy to my left and noticed he was still angry. I didn't want to create more trouble for myself, but how could I disobey a teacher?! So I stood there, stuck in fear, with this unfair lose-lose dilemma. After a long pause, I finally gave my answer. Looking down at the floor, my body tensed as I uttered the word, "no."

My skin cringed as I heard the teacher become frustrated and demand, "Hit him back the way he hit you!" I was afraid of the bully, but now I was more afraid of this teacher's wrath. With another long pause, I repeated my protest, "no." The teacher was now frustrated with me and told us that we would both stand here, until I hit him. Wanting this episode to be over, I raised my fist and tapped his shoulder with my left fist lightly. She raised her voice at me, insisting, "Hit Him Harder!." So, I finally did using my right fist. I punched him on his bicep as hard as I could. The boy immediately grabbed his arm with his other hand, and I saw tears fill both of his eyes, due to the stinging pain still throbbing. The teacher was satisfied with my punch. The school yard lesson was over. I stopped playing "out there" during recess after that

But soon I realized that the pre-school incident was STILL not my "First Educational Experience." Straining myself to think as far back as I could, I vividly remembered sitting on top of our small kitchen table, in our apartment on Virginia St around the age of three years old. My mom standing in front of me telling me to repeat these words in unison with her, *"uno por uno = uno; uno por dos = dos; uno por tres = tres; uno por cuatro = cuatro; uno por cinco = cinco;…"*

My mom taught me the multiplication tables, at age three the way she learned them, by repeating mathematics in her head hundreds and hundreds of times until memory retention occurred. If I close my eyes and focus on that memory, I can still hear my mom's encouraging voice, saying the multiplication tables, in unison with me in my head, encouraging me to learn more. "uno por uno = uno; uno por dos =…"

"People will forget what you say and do, but they will never forget how you made them feel." - Maya Angelou

DOMESTIC RIGHTS

One afternoon, my dad, my bro, and I were driving home on Story Rd. towards the East Side. We made a left turn on King Road; and, on my left I saw my mom running on the side walk!

I immediately yelled out to my dad and brother, "There's mom!."

My dad made a quick left turn into the entrance of Emma Prush Park and my dad got out of the car to ask my mom what was going on? I didn't hear much, but my mom pointed at a lady that was walking away very fast. My dad drove my brother and I to McDonald's to eat, but it felt as if though he was stalling on purpose.

When we finally got to our street, I saw two police patrol cars parked outside our low-income apartments. My dad didn't seem surprised to see them, so my brother and I stayed quiet and didn't ask any questions. When we entered the apartment, I saw my aunt and two police officers standing next to my mom, as she sat calmly at the kitchen table. Even though the police officers made me nervous, I relaxed the instant I saw my mom smiled at me. My mom was sitting down, holding a baby. Since we live in a little one-bedroom apartment I overheard everything. It turns out that a woman who knew of my mom's kindness, knocked on the door and then just placed her infant baby boy on our door-step. That's the reason why my mom was chasing after her on King Road trying to convince her not to abandon her newborn baby.

The lady chose my mom to care for the baby because my mom had earned the reputation of being a "Helper of Women." In all my years, I have never heard my mom say "no" to any woman in need. My mom actively role-modeled what it is to be a compassionate-giver. For example, my mom would always gather our used clothes to take to Mexico. Other times, I would overhear my mom on the phone for hours and hours, listening to women vent their tears of distress. My *jefita* would proceed to give plenty of "consejos"/advice, to women in desperate need of guidance.

Even though I don't prefer to "hear" the *consejos* for myself, I have to admit that it does work for those countless Mexican women who share the same belief system. Besides motivating then and providing emotional support, my jefita is a woman of action whom always volunteers her services to whoever needs help. For example, my mom will often literally sit at the kitchen table for hours and hours gluing hundreds of centerpiece *"recuerdos"* or my mom would spend weeks making colorful "roses" made out of tissue paper for weddings, baptisms, or *quinceañeras*. I've seen my mom commit to driving women's kids to school every morning free of charge to allow those moms to take on a new job. I've seen my mom commit herself to helping her new friends sell AVON or jewelery or cookies without commission. I've seen my mom over and over again offer emotional support and encouragement to women hesitating to apply for new jobs, by driving them there and giving them a "pep talk" to boost their confidence right before walking into the job interview. Whatever the problem, whatever the obstacle, no matter how serious the problem was, her response was always, "*Si Dios nos presta vida y salud, de un modo o de otro, a ver como le hacemos.*"

I believe my mom is one of those pioneers of her generation, as part of the "second wave" of the Women's Liberation Movement, boldly insisting and reminding other Mexican women, "¡Tienes Derechos Como Mujer! ¡Exígelos!" Those basic rights include every woman had the right to work; every woman had the right to spend their own money however she wanted; every woman had the right to learn how to drive; every woman deserved to live in a rented house; and convincing every woman has the strength and dignity to leave her husband if she was being abused physically or by infidelity, telling women on the phone, "*Tú puedes sola. ¡Yo te ayudo!*"

Long story short, my mom took care of that baby boy for about six months, until the biological mom came back with police officers and claiming and accusing my mom of refusing to give the baby back.

CHASING CENTS

"To laugh is to risk appearing the fool,
To expose feelings is to risk showing your true self.
To Love is to risk not being loved in return,
To live is to risk dying,
To try is to risk failure.
The person who risks nothing, does nothing, has nothing, is nothing, and becomes nothing…..
Only the person who risks is truly free." ." —Janet Rand.

The summer after my sixth grade year, my cousins scored a job as the *"paletero* man," selling Mexican ice-cream. We would go pick up the "paleta" push cart, early in the morning, on San Antonio Street. We would take turns pushing the cart and ringing the bells, "Ding, Ding, Gling, Gling, Ding, Ding, Gling, Ding." When my feet got tired of walking, I would sit on top of the "paleta" cart while my cousin pushed me down the street. We had to sell the "paletas" for one dollar each; but, to make a profit, I would sell the ice cream bars at $1.25 each to pocket that extra quarter. It never mattered however, because we would always end up eating all of our profit, whenever we would stop to rest under a tree.

Since we came from poor families, "summer vacations" represented free time to make money. There was no such things as a weekly "allowance" for us kids; so we were always looking for ways to make money. I often would get my "hustle" on by washing car windows at the Tropicana and King's Super parking lots or by helping people load their groceries into their cars for spare change, or by climbing into smelly, disgusting dumpsters to collect aluminum cans.

One day, I saw an ad in the "Potpourri" newspaper, offering a job for teens. I called and left a voicemail stating that I was a twelve-year-old seventh grader who wanted to work. I got a call back about two weeks later. The boss asked where I lived? He told me he would pick me up at 8 am Saturday morning. I sat by the window waiting. This would be my first official job ever

I saw a long white van creeping down my street. I was sure it was the boss looking for my address, so I yelled out to my mom as I ran out, "¡*Ya me voy amá*!" A white van with no windows on the sides rolled up in front of my apartments, and the sliding side-door opened. Eight other kids were sitting in the back, each holding their big, blue, plastic container. The boss introduced himself to me. His name was Ken. Ken would drive us to different cities, Gilroy, Campbell, Fremont, and Redwood City, drop us off at one corner of some random street then say to us, "Knock on every single door. Walk down this long street all the way until the very end. I'll pick you up in 2 hours." I would push the door bell, then wait. I never knew what to expect. Sometimes, older ladies would peek through their windows, take one look at me, then ignore me without answering the door. Other times half-dressed women would answer the door and look at me up and down, smiling, while I gave my sales speech.

Many times however, I would hear dogs barking behind the closed door. The owners would open the door and allow their dogs to charge towards me. The dogs small or big would bark at me and maneuver around me in circles trying to bite my legs. I used my blue plastic container as my "shield" against the bigger dogs. But against the small dogs, I would place the bottom of my shoes in front of the dog's face. Their small mouths would try biting me, but my shoe was too flat for the smaller dogs' to get a bite. And while I was doing this "Please don't bite me dance," I would stare at the owners with the expression, "Hello!!, get your freaking dog off me!" But the owners would stand there, hearing me deliver my sales pitch, as I stood on one leg or spinning in circles –"shield" container. I learned to say my sales speech super-fast, with these dog-owners. After several dog attacks, I stopped trusting people, and I would skip the houses with the signs, "Beware of Dog" or whenever I heard a dog barking inside the houses.

Gas stations were the best places to sell, because the customers had no choice but to stand there and listen to me for 2 minutes as they pumped gas. I sold a lot of my items at the AM/PM gas station on the corner of Tully Road and McLaughlin Ave - that is, until one customer went inside and complained. I was told by the owner to leave and not come back.

The most memorable experiences I had during this "all commission" job was the day all the kids in the van complained that they were hungry! So, Ken stopped the van in the parking lot at the shopping center on Capitol Expressway and McLaughlin Ave. Some of the workers went to McDonald's, some to Taco Bell. I stayed inside van, "messing" with one of my female coworkers. That's where I received my first hickey ever, on my neck, at age twelve.

All of a sudden, five of our coworkers ran back into the van and yelled to Ken, "Leave quick!"

Me and another cholo coworker jumped out of the van to see what was going on. When I stepped out of the van, I saw 15-20 gang members mean-mugging us. So, I got into my "cholo-stance," put my chin up, puffed out my chest, and with my arms spread out to my sides, I told the gang crowd, "Wutz'up then?!" All of them started to walk in our direction. By this time, the girls in the van and our boss Ken were yelling at me and my coworker to get in the van. We finally decided to get in the van. As we got back into the van however, the other kids in the back of the van began to yell out, "Go! Go! Go!." Everybody in the van turned around to look out the back windows. We saw about 10 of the gang members chasing the white van at full speed, with weapons in their hands. They began hitting the sides of the van with chains and sticks. Our boss sped off cussing and yelling at me and my co-worker for getting out of the van to challenge all of them, resulting in his van getting damaged.

Three weeks later, I told my boss, "I quit" and I opened the door, got out of the van, and walked to the 22 bus stop on King Rd. I was fed up and tired - tired and frustrated of working all day for no money. Sometimes Ken would give us five dollars at the end of the day, so that our moms would not get mad. But that still was not enough. I had more to lose than to gain; getting dropped off in random neighborhoods for 6 hours. For example, one time I was sitting in a Burger King on El Camino Real somewhere, when a cute girl walks up to me with a smile, and asks, "Where you from?" I gave her my usual answer with pride, "East Side San Jo." I then asked her, "What city is this?" She answers again smiling, "Redwood City." Then she says "Okay, bye" and exits the Burger King. I continue to eat my burger and fries. But I got a weird feeling for some reason. So, I decided to grab my burger and leave too.

Since I've learned to always trust my "Spider Sense," I walked fast towards the residential area. When I get about two blocks away, I look back towards the Burger King. Suddenly, I see twelve gang members running towards the Burger King and enter through the back entrance. And the same "friendly" girl who was flirting with me, was behind them. I observed them from a distance as they looked for me around the entire restaurant. Before they had a chance to exit and search their neighborhood, Ken drove up and picked me up. My gut-instinct has saved my "nine lives" many times.

CHAPTER II

SMALL FISH IN BIG SHARK-TANK

One cold winter morning, my brother walked me to the main entrance of Dorsa Elementary School. I was in 3rd grade and my brother was in sixth grade. As usual, I walked towards the back of the school, to see my brother walk by in the far distance on his way to Fischer Middle School. My inner happiness, innocence, and sense of safety departed from me this day. The cold feeling of fear entered my chest like a fog, and filled my hollow body, all the way down to my feet. I will never forget what I saw. I saw six arms swinging down at my brother's body as he bent down, covering his head with his hands. He was getting jumped and beat up by three guys. One big SamoanI still remember his name and two Chicano boys, around the same age as my brother. Twelve horrifying seconds later, I saw my brother break away from under the six fists raining down on him and run towards his middle school. Witnessing this unprovoked attack, caused my body to freeze. This was the first time in my life, that my feet became too heavy to move. I didn't know what to do. I felt so small—so weak. Allowing those three older boys to get away with that attack, gave birth of my anger. Anger at myself for not running up on them and stabbing them with my no. two-lead pencil, even if I was only eight years-old.

Because of these random attacks, my brother decided to join a gang for his protection. On the East Side, things only get worse, not better when you enter into a higher grade level in school. War stories are all I heard from my brother when I would ask him, "What happened at school today?" These reports painted a picture of what I should expect when I entered Fischer middle school. Instead of fearing gangs, I began seeking the power that gangs possessed. In 4th grade, I started my wanna-be gang in Elementary School. I called my group of friends, "D.F.G.—the Dog Faced Gremlins"—a name gained from watching wrestling shows on TV. A couple of girls in our 4th grade class became concerned at the fact that our membership was growing, so they told the teacher, the teacher then told the school principal. The principal walked into our classroom the next day and called me into her office. She sat me down and began her investigation, "I heard you started a gang?" I denied it Then she sternly stated, "We don't do that here." And she made some threat of what would happen if this small gang group continued—which scarred me. So that day the dog faced gremlins retired and were no more.

When I got to Fischer Middle School as a sixth grader, I knew I was now at the bottom of the food-chain. My brother was now in ninth grade at Overfelt High School. Just like my bro, I too saw several fights inside and outside the classroom. Because so many students carried weapons to school on the East Side, the Alum Rock School District sent letters home explaining to parents that regular "Jansport" backpacks were no longer allowed on school campuses. Instead, parents had to buy students a new type of "See-Through" plastic backpacks. That's right, Alum Rock Union High School District student now had to carry a dorky see-through backpacks made out of a thick plastic. I remember standing in a long line in front of the entrance of Fischer Middle School, waiting for the vice-principal to inspect the contents inside my backpack before being allowed to enter the school.

That year I learned a lot about the Law of Survival. We human beings are mammals according to Mother Nature. And as animals, we have primitive instincts programmed into our DNA for survival. All animals have the following four survival options to choose from when faced with danger, "Fight, Flight, Freeze, or Fold/submit." All animals must do a quick-second threat-assessment when a potential predator approaches. Unfortunately, false-pride of the streets teaches that it is more important to "win" a fight than to survive a fight. On the East Side, I learned that there is only one acceptable option when faced when faced with a threat- and that is to Fight, Fight, Fight, and Fight. If you choose Flight like deer who run away—you are weak. If you Freeze camouflage yourself like a lizard—you are weak. If you Fold turn your belly up in submission like dogs do—you are weak.

Back in fifth grade, I remember getting into a verbal altercation with a new kid on the block while playing soccer. We stepped up to each other and moved around in a circle with our left shoulders bumping into each other. This day however, I got a rude awakening and learned a valuable lesson about school yard fights. Instead of walking around in a circle looking tough in front of the other kids, this new kid decided to punch me instead on my left ear. I was stunned. I wasn't expecting that. When I took a step towards him, he punched me again on the nose! I stood there, huffing and puffing with anger, but frozen with confusion. I was not scarred of this boy, but I stood there looking like an idiot because I did not know how to fight.

Back in our gang infested neighborhood, older bullies began targeting my brother on our way to or from the grocery store. When they would approach us, I would try to make my body language look dorky or goofy, not tough, so they would leave us alone. I was choosing to "Fold" as my way to stay safe. I tried to convince my older brother to do the same, but my brother was learning to survive a different way. He was learning to "Fight" to make it through another day in the concrete jungle of ESSJ.

My brother was actively banging every day. Some days he would wear his "winos" black cholo-slippers to school. Those days, I knew to stay near the phone, because my brother would call me from a pay phone near Overfelt, and say to me, "Bring me my cortezes." I knew what that request meant. It meant that there was going to be a fight after school, and he needed his "war shoes" on. I soon began to see the world through my brother's eyes, and began to believe what he believed—that, "Offense is the best defense." But no matter how tough I wanted to be in sixth grade, the sad reality was that I was still a short, chubby, 11-year-old "paisa kid" with no muscles.

When I was in fifth grade, I felt more confident because I was in a small elementary school "pond." I loved playing soccer, dodge-ball, kickball, etc. But when I got to sixth grade, I quickly realized I was "a small guppie" in a larger shark-tank. I began to hate P.E., because I was either picked last or I would have to stand there listening to the "popular" team-captains argue with each other, "I don't want him, you take him!" I never felt so rejected in my life, especially when I would try my hardest to convince them that I was a valuable player. It was never good enough. After several weeks of this emotional torture, I lost all hope in my athletic abilities. I gave up and gave into the message of being "no good." As a result, from that day forward, I stopped smiling, I stopped laughing, I stopped playing sports, I stopped being a kid, I stopped being happy.

As a depressed eleven year old, I discovered that life can ALWAYS get worse. I remember the worst and lowest day of my sixth grade year. As I walked back home after school, I got the urge to go pee bad. I was still eight blocks away from home! There was no way I was going to make it! But there were no stores, no gas stations for me to use a restroom, only residential houses. I thought about peeing in somebody's bushes, but it was broad day light outside—No Way! I began walking fast, trying to get home before my bladder exploded! I was in the home-stretch - now only four blocks away. I had to concentrate, "Don't pee, don't pee, don't pee."

But of course, "Murphy's Law" came true this awful day. As I approached Dorsa Elementary School, two older

Overfelt High School vatos, probably in eleventh or twelfth grade, came up to me from behind. They were bigger than me, surrounded me, pushed me.

They asked me "What you claim!?"

I "Froze" again with fear, feeling that same cold air fill my lungs and chest. That frigid fog traveled down both of my legs, making them too heavy to move. Talk about the worst timing to get "hit up"!

With my stomach muscles trembling, I responded, "I don't claim."

I couldn't hold my pee anymore. They didn't notice, but I started to releasing some of my urine, feeling the warm liquid run down my right leg. At that point, I knew I had to get home asap before I completely soak my pants! So, I turned around and walked away hoping they wouldn't chase me. I think they felt sorry for me, because they just let me go. I never told anyone this embarrassing story. But I felt better, once I learned that zebras do the same, releasing their urine, to make their bodies lighter, a second before jumping away and fleeing from lions or other dangers. I felt even more relief when I heard Mike Tyson in a documentary tell his life story about how he always ran away from fights, and was also humiliated in the streets, growing up as a fearful kid.

The only time I ever felt safe or like I was somebody cool, was when I hung out with my older brother. Nobody ever messed with me around him or his older homeboys. I felt powerful being around their bold confidence. One afternoon, while my brother's gang met in the garage around the pool table, I volunteered to serve as "the look-out," riding around in my bicycle along Sunset St. looking for any police activity. The gang was waiting for the leader to call and give the order to rush Poco Way. As an eleven year old, I was always the tag-along with my older bro everywhere he went. Soon after, I became known as "Droopy's little brother." I wanted to make my big brother proud of me, even though I still dressed like a poor Mexican kid. I didn't look cool at all - with my "Pro-wing Tennis-shoes" or my "LA Gear air-pumps," but I guess that's why I made such a good "look out," because nobody ever noticed me. Just as the "tick-bird" serves as an effective "look-out" for Rhinos.

Early the one morning, my brother left home 1st to his high school. About forty minutes later, I put on my "square-bear" clothes, and dorky backpack, and I walked along the sidewalk of McCreery Ave towards Story Rd.—as usual. I never avoided walking past Poco Way for three reasons, I was not in a gang. I did not have any enemies, and lastly, I didn't dress like a gang member. Well, I learned a harsh reality this cloudy morning. I learned that just because I tried to avoid gangs, did not mean that gangs would try to avoid me.

As I walked passed Poco Way, I saw five high school age *Sureños* get into a small, dark blue, 80's model "hooptee." I kept walking trying not to make any eye contact. But, with my left ear, I heard one of them say, "Ay! That's that one puto's brother!." I kept walking, waiting and listening for any feet running behind me. But what I heard was much worse. I heard the car doors slam shut, I heard the car's engine rev up, and then I heard the tires screeching as they made a U-turn toward me. I looked back as the car spun around in my direction. I started sprinting. Although I was still half a block away from Story Road, I put my head down and sprinted as fast as I could on the McCreery sidewalk. I heard the car load of Sureños yelling and cussing from inside the car in excitement of their new found prey, as the car raced towards me. They didn't care that I was only in sixth grade, more than five years younger than they were. I ran across Story Road without waiting for the light to turn green. Luckily no cars hit me as I ran across the busy six lanes of traffic. I immediately ran into "24 Markets" Liquor Store. I looked out the windows, with my heart still pumping in panic. They stopped the car in the middle of the street, waiting for me to come out. After about 2-3 long minutes, they drove out of sight. Fearing that they were waiting for me around the building on Bal Harbor Ave, I waited a while longer, playing video games with one eye on the glass doors. I arrived tardy to school that morning.

    I realized now why my brother always carried a 17" inch long metal pipe up his right sleeve, under his right arm pit so he could just let it slide down into his right hand if he needed it. He also often carried a bike-chain with a pad lock attached at the end of it. In retrospect, the "Flight" instinct response helped me to survive that morning. When my brother got home school, I told him the "almost story" that had occurred. What he said next, I remember vividly because he said it with no emotion. With a serious and eerie tone in his voice, he calmly said to me, "You're known now." As if though he knew this day was coming. He knew I couldn't hide anymore. That my "disguise" of a dorky Mexican kid would no longer work. I was marked as a permanent rival to all Sureños. All of my brother's enemies - had now become my enemies. I inherited a war. My older bro was not worried at all, because he had anticipated this day - ready to teach me all he knew about street survival, during especially the gang war of the 1980's and early 90's. He concluded with, "You gotta hang out with us now." Four weeks later, I bought my first pair of black and white cortezes, 6 Ben Davis pants from San Jose Blue-jeans, and 5 V-neck shirts from T-shirt Plus at Eastridge, and I represented my "colors" every single day from that day on—no longer undercover.

"Do Not Scorn a Weak Cub, He May Become the Brutal Tiger." - Mongolian Proverb

"DROOPY'S LIL BROTHER"

My parents have always been "hard-core Catholics." My older bro and I got dragged to church two days per week. One year, we attended "El Sagrado Corazón" Church on the "west side."

One afternoon, my dad told my bro and I, "get dressed." So, we reluctantly got ready to go "somewhere boring again." While on the 280 freeway, my bro and I already guessed which church we were going to, so we just rolled our eyes in irritation and zoned out into silence. When we got to Willow Street, we noticed that the big church doors were closed and the lights inside the church were turned off. My bro and I felt relief until we found out the mass celebrations were being held in "the hall" next door, due to the structural damage caused by the big earthquake of 1989.

As soon as we saw the priest, my bro and I assumed the same'ol routine, so we "tuned out" immediately. But, for some reason, my natural curiosity didn't allow me to day dream this day. Padre Mateo Shinney, S.J. spoke in Spanish, but it wasn't the same mass verbiage as usual. Padre Mateo announced that his guest speaker was here to talk about something "very very important." The hall was packed past capacity. Older Mexican men and women sat on the cold folding chairs. The rest were standing against the back walls. An older Chicano man then walked up to the microphone and spoke for about forty-five minutes. At first the crowd of Mexican men and women were quiet, but soon the crowd began arguing with him, shouting frustrations, and demanding answers from this polite, gentle Chicano man. I don't remember the details of this debate; but I do remember two things very clearly, I remember the urgency and frustration in this Chicano man's voice, as he pleaded, "Tenemos Que!" I also remember the zeal and passion in this Chicano man's voice as he repeated his simple, yet profound message of, "¡Sí Se Puede!" "¡Sí Se Puede!," "¡Sí Se Puede!" as the crowd roared in applause at the end of the meeting - now motivated to do their part and join the protests and boycotts. Many years later, I would finally learn to appreciate and understand the honor and privilege I had experienced that evening—I had witnessed and heard Cesar Chavez speak live, within ten steps in front of me. When I think of César Chávez, I think of one word, Zeal. The dictionary defines zeal as "The Enthusiastic devotion to a cause, ideal, or goal and tireless diligence in its furtherance."

Sadly, as a short eleven-year-old, chubby kid at that time, I didn't admire, nor looked up to any adult leaders. My only hero was my older brother, that's why I always tagged-along with him no matter where he went. No adult leader spoke to me in my teen lingo. No adult leader understood the realities of my "Story & King" world. My bro did, so I followed his footsteps as my leader.

I was in seventh grade, when I attended my first gang meeting. These meetings were held every Friday evening at a local park. I used to climb the same tree and hang out there, serving as "the look-out" while the gang met to discuss business and jump-in new homeboys. From that tree I saw and heard everything, even though I pretended not to. One Friday, 15 homeboys stood in a straight line facing the shot-caller as he paced left to right in front them issuing his weekly orders, "I want to hear more war-stories every week from each of you!" Active gang-banging was expected from this gang leader.

The shot-caller then brought up his idea about purchasing V-neck shirts from Eastridge and getting the gang's name in Old-English lettering printed on the back—for members to represent.

I remember the shot-caller standing in front of each gang member's face and asked, "you going to pitching-in money to buy shirts?"

One by one, they each answered the same question with the same answer, responding, "Yeah," "Yup," "Simon," "Yeah," "Yeah," but then one of the newest member gave "his own" answer. Answering the "question" with an, "I'm not sure." At that moment, within one second flat, the shot-caller yelled out, "Get this fool!," so everybody instantly, without any hesitation, rushed him—punching and kicking this guy to the floor, continuing to stomp his body on ground for 15 long seconds. After they finished jumping him, everybody nonchalantly lined back up again. The new guy got back up on his feet, wiped the grass and dirt off his clothes and stood in line again with a newly inspired decision to contribute some money for shirts. The shot-caller, now pissed off, walked down the line and sternly mad-dogged everybody, barking the same question again in a loud voice, "WHO ELSE AIN'T SURE!?"

Everybody was now unanimously "sure" they could pitch in money to purchase the members-only "uniform."

One Friday, the president of the gang saw me chillen up in the tree and asked my brother to call me over. I climbed down. The gang leader asked me a couple of questions and then told me that I was welcomed to hang out with them anytime. From that day on, I chilled on the cement benches with them. They allowed me to tag my name on the cement picnic table with a big, black, "magic marker." A couple of weeks later, they handed me a red spray-can and encouraged me to "hit up" the outside wall of the public bathrooms, in broad day light. I didn't know how to tag "right" my first time, but I got better practicing on sidewalks, busses, restrooms, fences, and "the alley."

One of the last memories I have of these weekly gang meetings was "the debate" over me joining the gang or not. Half of them said that I should get jumped in now at age twelve. One older vato tried to convince me to join now, explaining to me, "Look, if you join us, you can act however you want at school. And if anybody talks shit or disrespects you in any way, call us, and we'll be there with the quickness and smash on whoever." That offer felt good because for the 1st time in my life I felt a sense of power with that much back-up - just a phone call away. Many "outsiders" don't understand that when you live in poor neighborhoods, we don't own many material possessions. All we have is our dignity, honor, and reputation, aka, "Respect" - which most live and die for.

The others half of the gang members debated that I

was too young to join the gang and that I should wait until I turned thirteen years old. I looked up to all of them. I wanted to be like them. I felt untouchable walking around with them. Hanging out with the gang was addicting. On weekends, we would mob-deep at Eastridge Mall - challenging the Samoans, and trying to spot undercover rivals wearing our colors. The cops and mall security would sprint over to intervene and tell us the same'ol warning, "Disperse."

During the summer, we often played tackle football at our park - "Shirts vs. Skins." That park was the only place I felt confident and powerful, because back where my bro and I lived about a mile away, we were surrounded and lived in enemy territory 24-7, always outnumbered 10,1, always the prey. The only negative memory I experienced at that park, was the day of the big rumble was scheduled in mid-March, during my seventh grade year. Waiting for our enemies at the park made my whole body so tense, that I experienced my very first "back muscle spasm," at age twelve. I didn't know what was happening to me, I just knew that all the muscles in my back cramped up so bad that it was hard for me to breathe or walk. I felt paralyzed. It felt like a huge giant picked me up in a permanent bear-hug that was crushing my back, lungs, and kidneys. It was the worst timing for me to get a "muscle spasm." I was worried I wouldn't be able to get away when the cops arrived. Regardless of the pain, I stood my ground at the park and continued to watch my brother's back as we waited. I couldn't wait to get to Overfelt High School—that's where my gang banging destiny awaited me.

"Be careful what you wish for - you might get what you want, but you might not want what you get."

TRUST NO ONE

Attending Fisher middle school in sixth and seventh grade, felt like "dead time" solitude. The only memorable experiences from my "Fischer days" were winning two art contests; having a seagull crap on my new sweater once; constructing a clip-board and tool box in my metal-shop class; getting into a "wrestling fight" during lunch-time in the field; and watching three girls sprint across the field, trying to out-run TABS the truancy cops.

The most boring part about Fischer, was SSR "Sustained Silent Reading". I hated SSR because I hated to read. Well, I later realized that it wasn't that I hated to read - I just really hated reading boring books! I'd always get bored and start tagging inside the book covers. Why? - Because those books never told My Story. An East-Sider's life never made it into the books at school. That is, until I found the book, "The Outsiders." This was a story of a teenage boy, nicknamed "Pony Boy." "Pony" was a poor kid who hung out with his older brother, and hung around older gang members like me!

When I got home that day, I saw an official looking letter from the Alum Rock School District on top of our kitchen table. Since my parents could not read English, I translated the letter for them. I didn't understand it; I mean, I didn't want to understand it. The letter said that the District's "boundaries" had "changed" — "What da!?" Many students at my school were also confused about the letter, so the teachers explained the new policy. The District now decided that if students lived on the other side of Dorsa, towards Story & King, we were now being transferred to Lee Mathson Middle School, starting in September. Students were in panic-mode and disbelief, because nobody wanted to go to Lee Mathson. Lee Mathson had a reputation. Everybody knew that middle school kids who got kicked out of their regular school, were all sent to Lee Mathson. Lee Mathson was a school for "throw-away" kids. My stress level elevated to a new high. Why? Because even though I was bored at Fischer, I felt safe at Fischer—especially since all my brother's homeboys were just a block away at Overfelt High School. Now, transferring to Lee Mathson meant no safety EVER!. Safety didn't exist for me in my neighborhood; and now, safety didn't exist at school either. I would be surrounded and outnumbered by rival enemies both at school AND at home, 24-7!

  Because of this fact, I began to plan. I told myself, "I refuse to go into Lee Mathson without guaranteed back-up." So, at the next gang meeting, I told the gang I wanted to get jumped in before my eighth grade began. I could no longer wait until my thirteenth birthday in December, I had to get jumped in before August. They all agreed. They told me they would initiate me as an official gang member in two weeks. I felt relieved. But those plans all changed one dark and eerie Friday afternoon.

  My gut-feeling told me something went wrong, especially when my brother didn't come home after school as he usually did. I looked out the window to see if any rivals were on our street, preventing my bro from getting home, by blocking his path - like many times before. To avoid the Poco Way Sureños, my brother and another homeboy Israel who lived in our apartments always chose the alternate route home. Most days, my bro and Israel would walk through "the alley" between King Super and the Pay'n Pack Warehouse undetected. Every day, I would look out our apartment window to see my brother and Israel and Israel's lady crossing Story Road on their way home from school.

One day however, instead of strolling across Story Rd, I saw my bro, Israel, and Israel's girlfriend jogging across Story Road. Suddenly, from the left side of my vision, I saw fifteen Poco Way Sureños, like the "running of the bulls" in Spain sprinting up our street to cut them off. I immediately ran outside to help. As I got to the sidewalk, I saw my brother and Israel punch their way through the crowd of Sureños then sprinted inside Israel's corner unit apartment. The fifteen Sureños remained outside, waiting for them in the middle of the street, so I went back inside our apartment to avoid getting rushed myself. As I looked out the window again, I saw my brother and Israel come back outside! But this time they were both holding huge machetes!

From our second story apartment window I observed ten of the Sureños pretending to "Fold," walk away towards Lee's Burgers. My brother and Israel began provoking them, by yelling, "Wutz'up then! Fuck you! Come on *putos*! LET'S DO THIS!" My brother and Israel began moving towards them, about to rush the entire mob of them. But what my brother and Israel didn't see was that fiveof the Sureños were hiding behind a parked car, waiting to ambush them from behind! I knew I only had 5-8 seconds before a full-on bloody rumble erupted in the middle of our street. So, I ran outside again, and yelled out to my brother and Israel "WATCH OUT!" and I pointed towards the vatos hiding behind that car! When the Sureños realized that their plan didn't work, all fifteen of them stood up tall and formed an offensive line, like a football squad as they got ready to blitz the three of us. I immediately pulled my brother from the back of his shirt and told him to get inside the apartment now! Even WITH machetes, three against fifteenvatos were not good odds.

    This is why, on this Friday evening, as the sun began to set in the sky, my mom, dad, and I worried like never before. They kept asking me if I knew where my brother was? I tried to keep them calm by lying to them—saying that he was at a friend's house. When dinner hour came and went, dad turned his worry into anger. After 3 hours of waiting with no sign of hope, I began to fear the worst, imagining my brother laying in the street bleeding somewhere by himself. Last time he was "caught slipping" by himself two blocks away in one of the back-streets, he was "sandwiched-trapped" from both sides by one car load and one van load of thirty Sureños. First they tried to run him over with a car driving on top of the side-walk and then the van load tripped him as he tried to run away. Those 30 fools stood over his body in a circle, and simultaneously stomped and kicked him repeatedly, while he was on the ground. With that image in my head, I had to go looking for him—out there, in enemy territory. So I went inside the apartment, grabbed my knife, and went on a solo rescue-mission. When my mom saw me come inside and leave in a hurry, she ran outside behind me. My mom caught up to me about two blocks away. She saw the knife in my right hand.

My mom began pleading with me in the middle of the street, with tears in her eyes and desperation in her voice, "*¡No m'ijo! No te vayas!*"

She was fearing one son dead, she didn't want to lose another. I barked my orders to her on the public sidewalk.

"*¡Vete para la casa ma! Ahorita regreso. Voy a buscarlo.*"

But she cried even louder, begging me, "*¡No m'ijo! ¡por favor!*"

Sobbing, as she feared both sons would never come home again. My heart broke at the sight of my mom crying in anguish. I always hated seeing and hearing her cry. Since I did not want my mom exposed to the same dangers in our neighborhood. I put my arm around her to comfort her and walked her home. I promised my mom I wouldn't leave again that evening, but I told her I would stand outside in front of our apartment so my mom could see me from the window and wait for my bro to arrive. I paced back-and-forth, on the side-walk, feelings stuck with anxiety and frustration because I couldn't leave. If I tried leaving again, I knew my mom would run outside there after me and be in danger too!

I began to beg to my Holy Mentor non-stop, pleading like never before to allow my brother to hurry up and get home safely. Our dad was waiting inside with the belt in his hand. Thirty slow minutes later I saw my brother, from two blocks away, turning the corner. My bro was walking slowly, pushing his bike next to him. My worry turned into anger at that moment, and I ran half a block towards him, yelling, "Hurry up! Dad is mad!." But I quickly shut up. Why? Because I saw a look in my brother's eyes and face that I had never seen before. He looked confused and sad. When I asked him where he was? All he said was, "Get me some pants." I looked down at his pants. He was wearing light blue jeans. But one side of his pant leg was no longer blue. The right side of his pant-leg was stained dark maroon with blood. I ran into the apartment, grabbed a pair of pants, and ran back outside. He changed downstairs, but when I heard my mom coming down the stairs, I hid the blood stained pants under the sofa cushions. She saw the suspicious look on our faces and she immediately looked under the cushions. I'll never forget the look of horror that came over my mom's face, eyes, and soul, when she saw the blood stained pants. Her worst nightmare had come true. With a waterfall of tears streaming down her cheeks she asked,

"¿¡Qué pasó m'ijo!?"

My brother and I wanted my mom to keep this a secret from dad, but she couldn't. My mom went upstairs and began to cry out loud.

"¡Le pegaron a m'ijo! Lo picaron!"

My dad called for my brother to come upstairs. When my dad examined my brother's leg and saw the deep stab wound, my dad's anger left him.

His only response was, "*Esto está serio. Tenemos que ir al hospital.*"

My dad put his boots on and drove my brother to the hospital.

It was a rude awakening for my parents. That night my parents had to face and admit the reality that their sons were actively involved with gangs. At the hospital, the doctor told my brother that they couldn't apply any stitches, because the stab wound was too deep, and it might already be infected inside. So the doctors refused to close up the wound. When the police officers arrived at the hospital to ask what had happened? My brother told them a lie. My brother told the cops that 3 dudes had randomly attacked him near Independence High School, but would not be able to describe anybody because it happened so fast. They believed him.

That night, I decided —I decided that I would take my chances alone at Lee Mathson—with no back-up. The only thing I relied upon from that point on was, "*mi filero.*"

"Mas Vale Solo Que Mal Acompañado" —*Mom*

EIGHTH GRADE

I now had to face the fact, that I would enter Lee Mathson middle school solo. My brother said he would introduced me to his best friend's lil' bro who was already attending Lee Mathson. My bro and I walked over to "the corner house" and I said wutz'up to "Bones." It was just me and "Bones" - watching each other's backs from that point on. One day, as "*Huesos*" and I walked home over the "cat-walk" bridge, we saw seven older rival gang members, posted at the corner of Sunset Ave and Cinderella Ave. From a distance we tried to avoid them, by making a quick left turn. We knocked on two homeboy's houses, but nobody was home. As we walked away towards our homes again, we picked up whatever weapons we saw on the ground. I picked up an iron rod, and Bones picked up a green-colored broom stick. As we got near sunset Ave, we slowed down to peek around the corner. But my big mistake again was not "expecting the unexpected"! Suddenly, their "look out" spotted me, and in less than a second, they all began charging towards us in full speed.

You see, in those days, you either rushed or got rushed "on sight." I put my head down and ran as fast as I've ever ran in my life. I could hear the sounds of six pairs of cortezes stopping on the concrete street behind me like a pack of savage wolves on the hunt. I could hear their voices—cussing and snarling ten feet behind me and closing in closer and closer by the second. Now, half ways up the block, I looked up and saw "Bones" sprinting in front of me. At that very instant, I saw "Bones" quickly turn his head to look back over his left shoulder and his eyes grew wide opened in terror, with an, "OH SHIT!" look-on-his-face. He then put his head back down and began to sprint even faster.

With that sight, I knew I was not going to out-run them. So, it was "do or die" time. Flight-mode was no longer working. I had only two options left for survival, to make a quick and sharp, ninety angle left turn and jump over the wooden fences between the houses; or I had to slam on my brakes, pivot with my left foot back, and blindly swing the metal rod with my right arm in hopes of hitting somebody's cranium. My friend was thinking the same thing, because 2 seconds later, "Bones" made a quick left turn, between two houses, and he began to jump the fences. I made the quick left turn too, and quickly looked back over my left shoulder. What I saw next confused the heck out of me. I saw an empty street, with no enemies in sight. I didn't stop though. I continued jumping the backyard fences, over and over again, because we didn't know if our enemies were also jumping fences next to us, trying to cut us off. When we finally got over to the other street over, we slowed our sprint to a moderate jog towards the same homeboys' houses. As I walked up to the door again, I grabbed the left side of my ribs, because the inside of my lungs were burning.

This time the homeboys were there. So we told them

what happened and the 3 of them immediately grabbed weapons and we got into their car to go after them. The fear now turned into anger and thirst for revenge. But they had all returned to their home-base of Poco Way. And we knew better than to enter into trap.

I believe without a doubt, that I came close to death this day. When I got home that day, I made a permanent "personal policy decision" to never to run again. Why? Because learned I was too slow to outrun anybody past two blocks. And even if I did, I knew I wouldn't have enough energy left over to fight and defend myself. Except for the time an older Sureño tried to run me over with his huge truck one morning. That time I did run and jump over the chain-linked fence into school.

"Es mejor que digan—'Aquí corrió' que 'Aquí murió'." - Mom

SAN QUENTIN

One morning at Lee Mathson, the vice-principal walked into my math class and called me outside. He told me that I had been identified as one of the gang leaders on campus. He asked me to please instruct my followers to stop tagging up the school's walls. I tried to convince him that I did not influence those youngsters because I didn't call any shots. He didn't believe me though. Two weeks later, the principal selected me, plus 11 other "gang affiliated" students to participate in a Gang-Diversion Program at San Quentin Prison. A well-respected gang veteran, who's still working with at-risk youth in San Jose, to this very day, organized this field trip. The goal of this intervention worker was to show at-risk teens the dangers and end-results of getting involved with gangs i.e., prison, in hopes that we would make positive changes to our minds and lives - while we still had time to do so. Before the field trip, we were given specific instructions about what not to do. One of the clear rules we received was not to wear any blue jeans pants because if there were a prison riot, the guards would shoot the inmates, who all wore blue jeans.

It was a cloudy the day we left San Jose. I was a bit uneasy, because I was on a bus with guys that I was "cool with" and greeted daily with a "wutz'up chin-up" gesture, but the fact was I didn't trust them, nor did they trust me for that matter. As we approach San Francisco on Highway 101, the rain began to fall. When we arrived at San Quentin Prison's main gate, the gang-intervention worker told us to make sure to obey the Correctional Officers. The storm clouds above were heavy with water. We walked quietly across the parking lot, in a straight line, with both hands behind our backs. The head C.O. in charge yelled out to us, "Stop!, Turn to your left! Face me! Now keep your mouths shut and listen!" The 12 of us stood there, facing the Correctional Officer with our hands behind our backs, looking at the San Francisco Bay behind him. I could see the cold ocean waves splashing towards us, just 20 feet away. As we stood there in silence, the storm clouds spilled out its water contents upon us. The 60 mph gusty winds caused the heavy rain drops to tap my face, cheeks, and forehead horizontally. The Correctional Officer stood there in silence, fiercely looking at us for 10-15 long minutes. Nobody dared move. The storm showers continued pouring down. All our clothes got soaked, everything was drenched - all the way down to my underwear.

Then the Correctional Officer escorted us inside the cement walls and divided us into two separate classrooms. There were three hard-core status inmates waiting in each classroom. These men explained to us that they were convicted felons sentenced to death-row. They said they were "Lifers" who would never again be permitted to walk the city streets or go home to see their families ever again. These death-row convicts signed up to participate in this Gang-Diversion Program, volunteering their time, to speak to us youth about the life choices we were making as teenagers. The death-row convicts told us they deeply regretted the mistakes they made and wished they could go back in time and choose to stay in school. These men explained to us, "Your homies are not your friends! Your mom and dad are your only friends!" In the next room, I could hear the slamming desks as they attempted to scare us, thirteen-, fourteen-year-old teens straight.

The gang-intervention worker who had organized this trip, sat in the class the entire time - hoping for the light bulb in your minds to go on. After each death-row convict shared his testimony of what life decisions landed him in prison. They verbally described a fictitious scenario to evaluate if we had learned anything from their personal life stories. They asked the entire class, "If your homies picked you up one day and while hanging at a party, one of your homies shoots and kills somebody. Would you tell the truth about who pulled the trigger? Or would you keep your mouth shut and spend the rest of your life in prison for a crime you didn't commit?"

They told us, "Be honest. Don't just say what you think is cool to say in front of your homies here. Be real. Speak for yourself only. Make your own decision." The convicts asked each student, the same question, one-by-one, "What would you do? Would you tell the truth?" One by one, each student began to answer the question that they were taught to answer according to the streets. One by one, each student answered, "Nope, I'm not a snitch." Most of the students said it with a straight-face, with an attitude of defiance, but a couple of students, I could tell wanted to tell their truth, but were afraid of what other students in the room would think. The convicts became angry and frustrated with the class because not even their own tragic stories and life sentence on death row was able to change a young, stubborn mind. T

he convicts protested in a booming roar, "I'M ON DEATH-ROW!! DON'T BE STUPID! YOU WANT TO BE HERE!?" One convict was so frustrated, that he grabbed the desk of a student still sitting in it, picked it up off the ground about ywelve inches high and slam it down again, and yelled in their face, "WAKE UP! THINK ABOUT YOUR MOM!!." They continued asking each student to choose, life on the outside? Or life on the inside? All those before me answered, "Hell naw, I ain't no snitch." I was the last one to be asked the same question, "Would you tell the truth to avoid life in prison?" Keep in mind, I had the advantage of observing all the responses before it was my turn. I was able to read their facial expressions and understand the reasons behind their frustrations. I didn't know much, but I did know that these felons had lived long enough to have acquired valuable wisdom.

"Everyone is a Teacher—If you Listen."—Doris Roberts

So, I chose to answer honestly, according to my morals and beliefs. I answered, "Probably. I know I wouldn't let a friend go to prison for something I did." At that moment, two Lee Mathson classmates turned their heads towards me and looked at me with disgust. But the three death-row convicts, immediately smiled, walked over to me and shook my hand and said, "that's right!." I could see these men were sincerely happy. Why?—because their efforts did not go in vain. ***Their Mess had indeed Become their Message,*** and somebody actually heard it. After two-hours of teaching and pleading with us to choose life not death, they finally saw a tiny glimmer of hope. On the bus ride back, we heard that the same thing occurred in that other class as well. Another student also answered, "Nope, I'm not a snitch," and was ordered by death-row convicts, "STAND UP!!" And the two felons proceeded to yell in the boy's face. But this "get-tough tactic," of course, didn't work. The boy stood there emotionless—stoic, as conditioned by the streets.

Realizing this, the third convict calmly walked up to the teenage boy, looked in his eyes, put his hand on the boy's shoulder, and asked him a simple, yet direct question, in a gentle and caring voice, "Where's your dad?" The boy was unable to hold it back and immediately began crying, sobbing as he released his inner pain. The death-row felon wrapped both his arms around him and hugged him as a father would, catching and carrying the burden of the boy's pain as in the movie, "South Central". The man then turned towards the class, still holding the boy's shoulders and announced his truth, with tears in his own eyes, "Real men do cry." Then he turned again to look at the boy and said to him, "I miss my dad too." The class ended with an applause.

It was a great field trip. I chose not to go to the 2nd field trip, which attempted to scare the "knuckle-heads" more by through the prison yard's mainline. I did not go because I was no longer resisting the message. I was now definitely "scared" to lose my future. I no longer needed any more "scared straight" interventions. I needed a mentor. The care and wisdom the men shared with us in San Quentin was sufficient for me to begin "kicking back," prioritize my values, and take less risks. Little did I know, that this "Aha moment" realization and decision to "choose life on the outs" and "do right" comes with a price.

When I walked back into Lee Mathson the next morning, I felt the vibe had changed. I got weird looks. I didn't understand why until I heard the campus grapevine report that 2 of the students in my classroom at San Quentin, began telling everybody, "Enrique's a rat!, Enrique is a snitch," because of the "wrong answer" I gave to a fictional scenario that was used as a hypothetical example by the San Quentin elders. From that day on, my stay at Lee Mathson went down-hill. I almost got into two fights that same week. I say almost because our girls got between us to hold us back. This tension remained the rest of the school year. I expected to fight one of those two dudes at some point. But, my error occurred when again - I failed to "expect the unexpected." I eventually endured two stab wounds from someone who didn't even attend the same school and wasn't even part of the original equation. To summarize, I was labeled a "snitch" and went through all of this shit because I answered the "What if..." scenario question differently than the rest.

Regardless of what occurred, I don't have any regrets. I am grateful to those men at San Quentin who helped me the way Tookey Williams has helped many, by sharing the message that it is ok to go against the crowd - and that a man often has to stand alone to stay true to his values and beliefs. I hope those men one day receive my sincerest gratitude for their genuine efforts to help an at-risk teen like me. Those wise elders will always remain a permanent part of my history, and earned their angel wings by blessing the narrow path that I chose that day.

" An intelligent person learns from their own mistakes, but a genius learns from the mistakes of others."- Anonymous

NINTH GRADE—SILENT EAST SIDER

Laying on my bed, drawing on a sheet of blank paper, I heard the familiar sound, *Hoooo-WeeeT, Hooooo-WeeeeT!* It was my homeboys' whistling our signal, alerting me of their presence outside. I got up to open the door, four of my homeboys walked into my yard.

Two of them walked in and in a serious voice stated, "There's a car-load of fools driving around the neighborhood."

I responded in habit, "Ok, let me grab my knife."

I reached between the bed mattresses and pulled out my *filero*. As we walked towards McCreery Ave and Cinderella, an older homeboy told two other homeboys to make a left at the next street and walk around through the back streets to cut the car off if they tried to creep around us. I continued walking with the other two homeboys straight ahead. I kept turning my head back, in all directions trying to spot the carload. When we got to our kick-back house, we all met up in backyard.

Two homeboys walked up to me and said, "Let's take a walk."

We walked around the side of the house. They both got right to the point.

"We're going to jump-in the new booty today since he keeps hanging around us, but we want you to start it off."

My answer was, "Alright, cool."

I immediately started taking off my necklace, rings, and t-shirt, and tightened-up both my shoe-laces. We walked back to the rest of them and noticed that the guy we were going to jump in, had no clue what was about to happen. The homeboys slowly got into position around him. This vato STILL did not suspect anything. I didn't believe in sucker-punching anybody especially a homeboy, so as I stepped up to him.

I told the vato, "Ay, get ready."

In other words, I wanted him to put up his dukes and get ready to box me and defend himself.

The older homeboy standing behind him said, "What! Don't tell him to get ready!" and socked him on back of the ear. *POP!*

The older homeboy wanted to add an element of surprise. The new booty looked shocked and confused, not knowing why we were "turning on him?"

Another homeboy noticed the look in his face as well, and explained, "If you want to keep hanging out with us you gotta get jumped into the hood."

He nodded his head in comprehension and agreed to accept this honor.

Next, everybody rushed him from all sides. The two oldest were punching his back and ribs on one the left and one on the right side; the youngest one was kicking him up his ass and on the back of his thighs; I was standing in front of him drilling the top of his head. I landed several punches on top of his skull, as well as a couple of upper-cuts to his chin and side-hooks to his ears, as he bent over to cover himself. As I punched, I thought to myself, "I could easily trip him to the ground," but his beat down would become ten times worse if

I did. So I decided not to; but, continued to deliver rapid fire jabs, bink-bink-bink-bink-bink-bink, to the top of his cranium.

The youngest one of us, stopped attacking him first - after landing about fifteen kicks. After twenty more seconds, I stopped second. However, the two oldest homeboys must have had some bottled up animosity towards him, because they kept punching and kicking our newest member for about two more additional minutes, tearing off his bloody shirt with each punch they landed. After they both stopped pounding his body, the newest member wasn't sure if the initiation ritual was over, so he still had his fists up ready for round two. But that was it—a four minute long jump-in. Everybody walked up to him and shook his hand in welcome. His nose was still bleeding, so he used his ripped up tank top to wipe the blood off his face.

I told him, "Let's go to my pad, I have an extra shirt there."

Walking down the street toward my apartments, I noticed he stood taller with his chin up. His body language changed completely, conveying loud and clear that he felt pride representing our gang hood and felt tougher for enduring a four minute beat-down by four guys.

When we got to my apartment-complex, he stayed outside and washed the blood off his face with the water-hose. I handed him the shirt, shook his hand, and he left towards King Road to catch the "double-duce" bus home. I walked back inside my apartment, shut the door, and continued drawing.

Before I went to bed, I creased my Ben Davis pants to get ready for school the next morning, at Santa Clara High.

The truth, Santa Clara High bored me. I didn't care about school, that's why I often grabbed the "bathroom pass," walked out of class, and walked down the hallways, blasting Eazy-E on my headphones. One day I walked by the "detention room" and saw my San Jonero homeboys chillen in there. I decided to hang out in there also. I was never "sent" to detention, I chose to go to detention during Spanish class because we never did any productive school-work. Even though nobody ever saw me doing school work, I had A's and B's in all my classes. Why? - because schools never challenged me.

The truth was I was always an "under cover school boy." I would often get bored in school, so I would talk to the girls, tag on the desks, or pass notes to others, pretending not to pay attention in class. I never carried a backpack or notepaper. But what my classmates never noticed, was that I never missed a homework assignment; and I was never absent with a 100% attendance record, even if I was sick. I carried my homework assignment, folded up into a square, in my left front pocket. When the bell rang at the end of each class, I would walk past the teacher's desk and place my folded up homework on her desk and walk out the door. I never fell below a 3.0 GPA from Kindergarten to tenth grade.

After lunch one day, I went to my locker and grabbed my Algebra book. Two female friends stunned! said loudly in disbelief, "YOU're in ALGEBRA!?" They were shocked because they only knew me by my reputation persona of *"Silencio"* known as the quiet "East Side vato" who always had a serious look on his face, would never talk, smoked weed, wore gang colors every day, stole from backpacks, messed around with lots of girls, and would randomly cut school even during finals week.

Later on that year, my dad told me he wanted me to apply to a different high school next year. I said "ok." I always tried to obey my dad, even if I didn't talk much to him. I told my teacher I needed help writing an essay because I was applying to some new high school called "Behlermin"? Or something like that. My English teacher's eyes lit up; but I still didn't understand why she was so excited for me. She said it was a great opportunity, blah-blah-blah. My dad told me that I had to get my grades up even higher. So, every day after school I would take two busses and travel to Bellarmine College Prep to receive extra tutoring. Two Jesuit priests, Father Steve Artiga, S.J. and Father Scott SantaRosa, S.J. helped me with my homework. They walked me over to the counselor's office Mr. Rob Suarez to borrow his computer for me to type my entrance essay.

I told them "This is going to take a while."

They asked "Why?"

I told them, "Because I don't know how to type with two hands, only with one finger."

And they smiled as they saw my right finger pointing down, going around and around above the keyboard trying to find the letter I was looking .

My dad would then pick me up from Bellarmine around 5 pm and we'd head back "over the tracks" - to the East Side. We never knew what to expect when we got off the 280 freeway, onto King Road. For instance, one day, our entire street was blocked off by about thirty cop cars. Our older homeboy who lived across the street, drove two blocks over to Poco Way, blasted at a youngster with a shotgun, then drove back two streets back home. A different morning, my dad heard some noise outside, but ignored it. On his way out the door to go to work, he saw our window screen frame was all twisted up laying on the ground. Somebody tried to forcefully break into our apartment during the night, attempting a home-invasion, by pulling off the window screen and flung it back about 5 feet without trying to be quiet. Another day, as my dad and I arrived back home, we walked up to the front door and saw two deep screwdriver marks dug into the wood of both the top and bottom locks. Needless to say we never felt safe "coming home" nor "leaving home."

When I got older and started to drive, my mom or dad would call me on my cell phone and tell me in Spanish, *"Todavía no llegues. Hay muchos vatos en frente de la casa."*

So, I would have to figure out something to do for an extra hour or two before I headed home. When I finally decided to go home, I would drive past my apartment first, then I would drive past my homeboy's house to make sure everything was cool there, and finally drive around the block again to make sure it was safe to park. After patrolling my block twice, I would park my car, look outside all my car windows, grab whatever weapon I had accessible and silently walk to my front door, watching my back 360 degrees, listening to any dry leaves cracking on the ground. The worst part was walking through the apartment's garage-ports, because there are many hiding places for a potential ambush which made me nervous. So, I would walk to my apartment door every night with a fully-extended knife in my right hand. Once I was inside the front door, I'd relax.

Nobody knew the internal turmoil I was going through every day. I couldn't concentrate in school because I was worried about my friends and family back in my neighborhood and I always felt guilty not being able to protect them 24-7. I felt stuck in the middle of two completely different worlds. I felt only two emotions as a teen, anger and loneliness. That's why I would day dream daily or go to the movies so much because I wanted to escape my present reality. The only thing that ever changed was the girls I would meet on the bus each week. With or without them, I felt hollow inside - like a stranger was operating my body. I trusted no one. I didn't see the point to going to school every day, because every time I tried to envision a future past eighteen years old, all I saw was a wall of fog. Deep down inside my soul, however, I refused to accept despair. My soul demanded purpose.

As I sat at the double-duce bus stop, waiting for the city-limo to take me to school, a Missionary walked by and handed me one of those colorful booklets, and stated eight words, "All the Answers are In The Good Book," and he walked away. For the first time in my sixteen years, I felt hopeful and excited that I could find the answers I was longing for. When I got home, I asked my dad if we had a Good Book in the house? He said yes, but it was in Spanish. Since I couldn't read Spanish well, I asked my school counselor, Rob-dog Suarez, where I could buy one? He said he would look into it. The next day, he surprised me by giving me a brand new "New Testament." I thanked Rob and I started reading it non-stop, hungry for guidance, and eager to feed my soul. The truth, the words in this Good Book DID talk to me and I began to awaken. My first epiphany was confirmed while on the "Kairos Retreat." I looked back at the past four years of my life and I realized that I HAD changed. Bellarmine had provided me a safe cocoon for me to transform myself from the inside out. I realized Mr. Suarez saved my life by pulling me out of class often, listened to me, and pulled me into a future with hope. He would allow me to talk as long as I needed to, usually over an hour. He knew I had nobody to talk to. He knew that I was putting up a front to the rest of the world. He knew that I felt confused and lost.

He knew I had a lot of anger in me due to feeling like a victim. While on Kairos, he wrote this letter to me, *"To 'El Silent One'. ¿Qué pues vato? ¿Quiubo of my uncles. They were good men, like you. And like you, they grew up in tough times and tough places.*

What saddens me about them all but one has died is that they were very lonely men and never really let anyone know what was in their hearts. I know that they were men who did not believe that there was anything special about their lives, that perhaps they had very little worth as persons. So I wonder sometimes, 'Is it like that for Silent One?' I do not know the answer. You share much with me and your honesty honors me. You have come to me and sought my advice when 'pensabas en conseguirte un cuete, ¿te acuerdas?' But I worry about you. You know how to be kind and respect people, both men and women. But you also have a demon in you that pushes you to be aggressive and use people without regard for their value as persons.

You have a unique opportunity to help other people. I am so proud of the courage with which you speak, the directness...There is much wisdom in you and great compassion. Never be ashamed of the tenderness and goodness in you. I know it doesn't fit well in the Barrio, but even your homeboys are in dire need of it. Be strength for your values, for your family, for all people. God has much work for you, Vato. Let Him work through you. Let Him give you the love he has for you. Do good. Do what is right. —Paz y Cariño, Rob Suarez January 14, 1997"

Mr. Suarez convinced me not to buy a gun at 15 years old, which was good advice. "Rob-dog" would give me side-hugs as an expression of affection and friendship, which I didn't know how to receive, because I wasn't used to that. He would invite me to taquerias to eat. He taught me how to drive using his car.

He gave me his house phone number and said to me, "Call me if you are ever in trouble—day or night, I'll pick you up."

He went beyond his regular "school counselor" job description. His "go the extra mile" mentoring style, became my mentoring style, because it worked for me. While I was in college, I went back to Bellarmine to visit him. His door was closed. So I left him a note under his door like I usually did.

I asked the receptionist, "What time is Mr. Suarez coming back?"

She informed that he had gotten sick and was in the hospital. A week later, Rob died.

"To the world, you may only be one person. But to one person, you may be the world." —Bill Wilson

TENTH GRADE—CATCH 22

I always felt like a stranger or "visitor" at Bellarmine. It's weird, I would feel most "comfortable" as soon as my bus crossed over the highway 101—and I entered the East Side. The more I thought about my friends back home, the more I hated Bellarmine. A big part of me wanted to sabotage my education and transfer back to ESSJ. For two years in a row, I stopped studying for my finals. One morning, as I walked into my classroom and sat down, the Religion teacher announces a pop quiz exam. The teacher handed out the tests, and the students immediately lowered their heads to read each question. The classroom was super quiet. All I could hear was the sounds of pencils and pens writing answers down on two dozen pages. Since I didn't study, and I didn't feel like pretending like it did. I sat there in silence for ten minutes.

Suddenly, all the pens and pencils stopped, and heads and eyes turned towards me as they began to hear the sounds, "shhred, shredd, rip, rip, rip, rip, rip, rip, rip, rip, rip, rip"... I began tearing up my exam in front of everybody including the teacher, because I didn't see the point in handing in a blank exam back to the teacher. The teacher, sitting at his desk just looked at me in shock. Nobody dared open their mouths. They knew I was full of anger, ready to explode on anybody who gave me the pleasure of an excuse.

A week later was my U.S. History Final. I didn't study for that final either. This time, instead of ripping up the exam and being bored the rest of the hour, I decided to entertain myself with the questions. For example, one of the questions on the Final Exam, was, "Please define 'Catch 22'?" I didn't know the "correct" answer, so I wrote down my answer. I wrote, "I 'Catch 22' every day after school on The Alameda going East-bound." I didn't get a good grade on that final exam, but I didn't care. I wasn't happy at Bellarmine. But the truth was, I wasn't happy anywhere. I wondered what the world was like beyond 95116? Beyond 95127? Beyond 95122? I said to tell myself, "Things would be way better if I lived in Mexico."

Believing the grass was greener over there. But, when I went to Mexico, I felt bored. "What do I do now!???" Nowhere I went, did I find my "happy-place" waiting for me. Happiness was beyond my reach. Not even in my sleep could I rest, because I would have nightmares about 3-4 times a week, non-stop for about five years.

The "Twenty-Two" was my space shuttle escape. Escape from a fate I did not want to accept. Escape from the fate of long-term incarceration. So many of my friends and school mates walked the edge of addiction and were either pushed in or pulled in; so, I knew I had to create distance for myself - away from that edge.

But at this time in my life, I believed the earth was flat, so when I would get on the "double-duce," the furthest I would get to was Sunnyvale on El Camino Real, because "the fear of the unknown wall stopped me, and forced me to get off the bus, cross the street, and head back to my confines." If I couldn't see the tan-colored east foothills, I felt lost.

So, what I did was, I would go on "Bus Missions" all day. I would take the bus early in the morning, ride on it all the way up to that "invisible wall," and then take the bus back to "home base" aka "Eastridge Mall." The 22 bus also represented "Opportunity" for me. The 22 bus stop offered at least 15 minutes of "talk time" to "mack on" a cute girl, and it also offered at least thirty minutes of "talk time" with a new girl while riding on the bus. That's how I met most of my "bedroom buddies." And if one 22 bus did not have any cute girls in it, I would often get off the bus and wait for the next one, since every time the bus driver opened the double doors, it felt like opening a "fortune cookie." Although most days my only "mission" was to achieve sexual-conquests, deep down inside I was also keeping hope alive—hope of one day meeting "the one" by "accident" like in all those romantic-comedy movies, like, "Serendipity." But of course, I tried to push the hand of destiny to work a little faster, because loneliness is a painful companion. I suffered with my illness of loneliness for many years, because I did not know how to transition to, "peaceful solitude."

One morning, our teacher told the class, "We're going to the Chapel today." I thought "Whatever - same crap, different day." The Jesuit-Teacher told the class to either sit on a chair or lay down on the carpet floor for a guided-meditation session. Most of the students immediately chose the floor. I chose a spot on the carpet floor towards the back of the chapel away from everybody. As I lay there, I realize that there was no dangers there, so I decide to close my eyes and listen to the priest's words and voice. Father Allender put on a CD of actual ocean-sound waves at a beach. I listened to his instructions as he taught us how to relax our minds and body's by taking deep/slow breaths. My body felt relaxed. For the very 1st time in my life, I experienced and felt peace - to the point where I fell asleep. After that I felt hungry for more solitude, because within that private place of inner peace, I was able to see more, hear more, analyze more, and understand the difference between logical intelligence and the subtle moments of wisdom.

I realized that the problem wasn't how boring the little town in Mexico was; the problem wasn't the dangers of the East Side; the problem wasn't even Bellarmine - the problem was me. I had no peace inside of me. The grass wasn't greener "over there." In actuality, **"The grass is greener where you water it!"** - *Neil Barringham*. Because the only thing that My Mentor promised me was "Daily Bread." That's it. If I wanted anything else beyond that, I needed to build it. So, I made a terrifying choice, I decided to grab "the wheel." I decided to take control of my life. Rise or fall—it was now up to me. I decided to take hold of the "author's pen" and write my destiny.

RUN UP OR SHUT UP

"You ain't shit…" The 6'1" white boy said to me during art class. For the past three weeks, we both had been "clowning" on each other. But with those three little words he chose to utter — "se pasó" he crossed the line. At first, I tried ignoring him because he was known to run his mouth a lot. But the battle within me had begun. The lava beneath the surface had begun to flow, for the first sign of a tsunami approaching is the waves being pulled back from the shore. Ultimately, however, it was still my choice, 1. Do I let him slide and stay in school? or 2. Do I "handle it" and get kicked out of school? I had to think about it, It was my senior year in high school. I had already put-up with Bellarmine for three long years! If I get kicked out, all my hard work and sacrifice would have been for nothing, just a big waste of time.

But this fool did not know where I was from - where I'm from "you don't play like that." Earlier that year, I had made another white kid fly for the same type of offense. What people didn't know was that since I lost my last fight in 8th grade, I didn't feel confident in my fighting abilities. So I wondered if I would lose again? Since this guy stood six-foot-one, and bragged about knowing "kickboxing." I was 5'6" on a good day with no kickboxing abilities. So, I decided to ignore the comment.

However, the next day, as I was walking into History Class, this same asshole stood in the middle of the door, blocking my entrance. I told him, "Move." He said, "Make me." I responded with, "Just move fool!" He decided to move only half ways, so I pushed him entirely out of the way with my right hand. He then made his final mistake. This white boy got brave, and said out-loud, "That's what I thought! You can only push me from behind!" I proceeded to walk to my seat. He walked over to me in front of the entire class and continued saying, "See, i knew you ain't shit!" As he finished uttering those words… - I smiled. I smiled because I had "clicked over" to Silent-mode.

A student sitting next to me asked, "What's going on?."

I simply stated, "Don't worry about it."

During lunch, I went to another class to make-up a test. As I sat in the classroom, I saw the same tall white boy walk into the same classroom as me, to re-take the same test. I knew this was my window-of-opportunity. I finished my test fast, and I walked out of the class. I waited by the stairwell, knowing he would exit that way too. I tightened my shoe-laces, took off my T-shirt, leaving only my white tank-top on. As I cracked all my knuckles, I saw a cool classmate walk by.

I said to him, "You might want to stick around, if you want to see a fight."

He said "Ok," and stood by to watch.

When the 6'1"white boy walked through the double-doors, he looked at me like a deer caught in headlights. I walked straight up to him and socked him once in the face with my right fist "Bam!"

He was stunned by the assault and battery I had just committed, and he said, "What the Fuck!?"

I responded with my challenge, "Wutz'up then!? I'm right here!"

I waited five seconds allowing him to take off his backpack. Once his backpack hit the floor, I "took flight" on him again, landing rapid non-stop right punches to the left side of his face. His back was against the wall, as I "binked" on him with 15 solid straight punches. He landed only one punch to my left cheek. After 20 seconds, I stopped, and I took a step back. He decided to walk towards me and swing at me with a right hook. I blocked his punch with my left forearm, and I countered it with a heavy right fist to his face—"Boom!" At that moment, I saw both his eyes roll upwards to the back of his head and I saw only the whites of his eyes. His body leaned back like he was going down in a technical K.O. So I stopped. I threw the first punch, but I also threw the last punch. I finally unleashed the many years of bottled up anger and hate upon this student in 30-second of fury. The truth is, I stopped swinging because I scarred myself. I wanted to hurt, but I learned I didn't want to kill. I didn't realize the power of my punches, since I had never gone "full force" on anybody before, especially when jumping-in a homeboy.

When the teachers arrived, I didn't try to get away nor deny what happened. I just sat down on the floor and waited for my consequences. The guy I had just rocked, continued talking shit, even though the entire left side of his face swelled up nasty, turning different colors, black, blue, and purple.

For the record, I never saw a single kick from this so-called "kickboxer." I was suspended for the rest of the day.

I went to school the next morning to "face the music." Since I had never been a behavior problem at school, the dean told me they were not going to suspend me, but that I would be put on "disciplinary probation" and that I needed to write an apology letter to the victim and his family. I was also given thirty hours of community service. The next day, I was called into my counselor's office. The guy I fought was sitting in there, with dark sun glasses on, because his left eye was swollen-shut. I knew we were called in there to do a "conflict mediation," so, we both apologized to each other and "squashed" our conflict. But, my counselor still looked nervous and worried.

So, I asked, "What?"

The white-boy explained to me that his parents wanted to "press charges" against me for the aggravated assault and battery. He said that his parents also wanted me to pay for all the hospital bills, because according to the doctors, I had broken his eye socket. The worst part, as my counselor explained, was that there is a possibility that this boy might be permanently blind from his left eye. I was in shock and a daze, not knowing how I would ever explain this new reality to my parents?

The doctors told the boy to come back to the hospital in two weeks, after the swelling went down, to check for any permanent damage to his eye-sight. Those two weeks were the longest and saddest days of my life. I felt depressed realizing that I might go to juvi-hall; realizing that my parents might have to pay thousands of dollars in hospital bills; realizing that I wouldn't get to graduate high school, and worst of all — realizing that my parents' hopes and dreams of me going to college were now going down the drain. I realized I had unjustly made this Bellarmine kid pay for all those who had ever wronged me in the past. That violent attacked was intended for somebody else, not him. During those two weeks, I finished my community service hours and I begged my Higher Power/Mentor to allow this kid to see again. I didn't care if I went to Juvi, as long as I knew that I didn't cause any permanent blindness to anyone. My counselor Rob hugged me as I sat in his office stoic and numb. He told me that no matter what happened, he would be there by my side — to defend me if the school tried to expel me, or to show up in the courtroom to testify on my behalf or to visit me while in Juvi.

Fifteen long days after my volcanic-explosion, I got a note during class to report to my counselor's office. Rob-dog asked me to sit down. Rob said that the doctors concluded that the boy's eye sight would fully recover! I was so happy, that I smiled "with my teeth." Rob said that the boy's parents had also read my sincere apology letter and had taken pity on me, and that they had decided not to press legal charges against me. After this experience, I learned many truths about myself. I learned that I do not like hurting other living beings. I learned that I truly do value my education, my freedom, and my future. I realized that I truly felt real guilt and real remorse because my soul protested that act of violence that I committed. I realized now, that deep down inside, "I'm a lover, not a fighter."

"My life is in the hands of any fool that makes me lose my temper." —Joseph Hunter

NEW YEAR, NEW START

"Everybody truly dies, but not everybody truly lives." — *Prince Ea*

Most people go out to party to welcome in the New Year. For my family and I, New Year's Eve meant turning off all the lights, and laying down on the living room floor to watch TV. My parents would go to sleep early around 10 pm, but my brother and I would always stay up to wait for the clock to hit 11,50 pm. New Year's Celebration always started at 11,50 pm. Why? Because that is when the 1st gun shots would be heard firing up into the night-sky. But at 12am-midnight, every person in the neighborhood who owed a gun, began pulling triggers. "Pop!, pop!" from the revolvers, "tat!-tat!-tat!-tat!-tat!-tat!"from the semi-autos, unloading their clips, "boooom!" from the 12-gauge shotguns, and "pop!, pop!" again from a revolver. The variety of gun-shots would always begin ten minutes before midnight and continue no-stop until twenty minutes after midnight. I'd fall asleep every New Year listening to that "East Side Melody."

Around 9 am the next morning, I put on a hooded-sweater and walked two streets over to visit my best friend's house —"Bones." His house was the official "kick-back house." The homies would always hang out there. We'd meet up with girls there, order pizza to eat there, lift weights there, jump-in homies in his backyard there, or chill out front of his house, sitting on an old sofa/couch scanning cars roll by. As I walked over that morning, I saw my best friend from a distance standing outside his garage smoking a cigarette. I smiled as I approached, but he didn't smile back.

Confused I asked him, "Wutz'up?"

With a serious look on his face, he took one slower-than-usual drag off his cigarette and pointed one finger to the broken window on the side of his garage. As I looked directly under the window I saw a hole on the wall.

I asked again, this time with a serious tone in my voice, "What happened?"

He said, "They shot up my house last night."

Luckily, my best friend and his entire family were not home during the "walk-by shooting." Good thing his family was out of town visiting relatives for New Year's. As we looked around his house, assessing the damage, we counted at least eight entry points. Bullets hit his garage windows, the outside walls. The bullets also went through his mom's bedroom window and made holes in her bedroom walls. This was New Year's Eve on our side of town.

HOME-SICK

My first car was an '89 Pontiac. I loved the adrenaline rush I got when I'd speed down the 101 freeway, maneuvering past "slower" cars. I would drive so fast, that the little red indicator would disappear down past the 120 mph slash-mark.

Because of my immaturity, I didn't know how to take care of a car, so my Pontiac broke down on me often. I remember it would break down on me everywhere. One time the motor turned off while I was on the 87 freeway, so I had to walk down Curtner Street, towards Monterey Highway, catch the bus and continue to my destination. From that day on, I decided to buy an old 10-speed bicycle, and made it fit into my backseat. I would drive around the entire city with a bicycle across the backseat of my car, every single day. The next time that my car decided to break down, I simply opened my side door wide-open, pull the front seat forward, pull out my bike, and start pedaling towards my job, school, or home.

Sometimes, I would arrive to class at Santa Clara University, lean my bike up against the wall, and sit way in the back. Why? Because I discovered that I would start sweating about five minutes after I sat down, and I would continue sweating for ten minutes straight, as my body tried its' best to cool down.

Back at school, I got "a case of the Fuck-its" since I got rejected by the SCU Latinas on campus. So, I decided to seek out the "hood-rats" I knew all too well. Also, since most of my homeboys were "on the run," I would pick them up in my Pontiac and drive them to my "pad" at SCU's Swig Hall. We'd play pool, lift weights, eat pizza, and bring girls over to my dorm room, which functioned as a "mo-mo." The campus was always too intimated to ever say anything. When we weren't at SCU, we'd "mob deep," all over the city. I was always "the get away driver," "mashing out" whenever the situation called for it. I stopped caring about my future again. I activated my "I don't give a Shit" attitude. I would walk around the SCU campus and classes with a large knife, exposed in a black sheath on my belt. I would wear a white tank top, creased-down Ben Davis' cut-off shorts, white knee socks, black "winos" slippers, a black beanie on my head, black locks over my eyes, and hickies all over my chest, shoulders, and neck to class.

Since I had "females" living in enemy territory, I asked one of the homeboys for a *"cuete."* Because I was so paranoid, every time somebody knocked on my dorm room door @SCU, I would peek through the peep-hole holding a fully loaded .22 semi-automatic pistol in my right hand. I remember getting paged during class, "911-13-22," which meant "Homeboy Emergency-Enemies involved-Bring the .22 pistol." When I would get those pages, I would immediately run out of class, get into my car, and speed over to the East Side to back-up my homeboys. I gave the *"cuete"* back a month later because I knew they needed it more than I did.

I continued feeling "out of place" at SCU. Too many times I was singled-out unfairly and approached by SCU employees with the same ol'question, "May I help you?" with the unmistakable tone in their voice message of, "You don't belong here. Why are you trespassing?" I got home sick. The "SCU Bubble" made me sick to my stomach. I started missing home. I missed my mom and dad's home-cooked meals. I looked forward to moving back during summer vacation. But my parents were not as excited about my return to *"este lado."* My pops told tell me that enemies had been coming to our apartment, about once a week, looking for me. My dad said that I should instead look for a room-for-rent somewhere in the City of Santa Clara. I didn't want to do that, but my dad insisted that it was not safe for me to return home, especially since neighbors had recently reported that they had seen one of those enemies carrying a chrome-plated semi-automatic handgun.

    Since I didn't fear those fools, I didn't look for a place. So, on the last day of class, I packed all my stuff into my Pontiac and drove home—to the East Side. As I arrived at my parents' street, I saw three enemies walking by. I parked my car in front of our apartments and grabbed some boxes to carry in. As I crossed the street, I noticed that the three enemies spotted me. "On sight," they made a 180 degree turn and started to walk towards my direction. I walked inside the apartment calmly, greeted both my mom and dad with hugs and told them I was going to bring in more stuff from my car. At that point, my mom looked out the window and saw the three trouble-makers waiting for me outside. My mom yelled out to me, *"¡M'ijo! Espera!"*

"*¿Qué?*" I replied.

My mom ran down the stairs quickly, before I was able to open the door.

She whispered to me, "*No Salgas. Allí están afuera.*"

My mom saw my look of anger in my face and saw me take a step towards the door, and she reaches out to grab my shoulder pleading with me.

"*¡Espérate m'ijo!*"

At this point, I'm still downstairs, by the door, with my mom trying to convince me not to go outside, since she knew that the result would be all-bad if I "got down" with all three of those fools. My dad knew I was on the edge of losing my temper, so he called the police.

After making the call, my dad told me, "*Ya llamé a la policía.*"

My mom was now panicking and started to cry. Seeing her stress, I reassured her.

"*Okay, no voy a salir.*"

And I sat down on the steps and waited, still pissed off at those cowards who didn't know how to fight fair.

A few minutes later, I heard four knocks on the door, THUUMP!-THUUMP!-THUUMP!-THUUMP! and a loud voice stating "San Jose Police Department!"

I opened the door and a police officer asked me if I lived there.

"Yes, I'm moving stuff in," I said.

As I went out to my car to get my stuff, nobody was out there. I guess another cop car had chased the three guys down the street. I got the rest of my stuff out of my car and carried the boxes into the apartment. The police officer was now asking my dad questions. My dad saw how pissed off I was and told me that he didn't want me to stay there because he knew sooner or later I would clash with those enemies that lived only one block over.

"Do you want him to stay here?" The cop asked my dad.

I stood there with two boxes in my arms waiting for his answer. My dad told the cop it was too dangerous for me to stay there.

"Hurry up. Grab whatever you can carry and get back in your car." the cop said to me. The cop stood there, by the trunk of my car, and waited until I left. My "return" back home lasted only twenty minutes. I wasn't mad at my dad. I understood why he did what he did. But this incident only fueled my internal fire.

I drove twenty minutes back to the city of Santa Clara. I looked for a quiet residential area, parked next to a wooden fence, wrapped my sweater around my tennis-shoes as a pillow, and I slept in the back seat of my car that night. I found a room for rent the next day in Santa Clara. I was mad as hell, because I was "homeless" once again. It hurt me not being home and I knew it hurt my parents too. When I spoke to them over the phone, my mom would verbally remind me every single day,

"*No te vengas para este lado. Quédese allá m'ijo.*" Don't come over here to this side. Stay over there son.

"Rules exist for the obedience of fools and the guidance of the wise."—Douglas Bader

LOST AND FOUND

"Home is where the Heart is—the place with Heart"

My life began falling apart. I was far from home—alone. All my homeboys were incarcerated during this time and my parents didn't want me going home because of safety issues. So, every time I looked over to the tan colored East Foothills—I missed my home. To cope with the loneliness, I worked more and called ex-girlfriends. But those visits never fixed anything. So, I began going to the video stores and rented three movies every three days and ate junk-food. The more home-sick and lonely I got, the angrier I got; and, all that anger bottled up and spilled over into "road rage." I began "punching" the gas pedal every time the red light turned green. My impatience and irritability grew so much that I would often "run red lights." As a result, my Pontiac's transmission broke down. I quickly learned that "When it rains it pours," as "Murphy's Law" states.

Spending all my money on, car repairs, bicycle repairs, movie-rentals, fast-food, and the room I was renting - left me broke. Since my mom always worried about me, I committed to calling her once a day to reduce her fears and reassure her that I was safe and o.k. But what I never told my mom was that sometimes I had to "pan-handle" from strangers to collect enough coins to call her from a pay phone and bus fare, since my car was stuck at the mechanic's. During those long weeks that I didn't have a functioning car nor bicycle, I would walk. The room I rented was located a block away from El Camino Real off Kiely Blvd.

I had to wake up at 5 am, get dressed for work, and leave my room at 5,30 am to get to my security job by 7 am. As I walked along the residential neighborhood, I noticed it was still dark and cold, almost "night time" at 5,30 am. The back-streets were pitch black, so I would walk in the middle of the street, because I was afraid of attackers jumping out from behind a dark bush, parked car, or a house. When I got to the main street Bowers Ave, I saw an older woman walking ahead of me on the side walk. She turned around, noticed me, and seemed afraid as she put her head down and continued walking faster. What she didn't realize is that I was also concerned for her safety, and I was keeping an eye out for her, "watching her back" from a block away. But I decided to cross the street to the opposite side on purpose to reduce her fear of me.

Fear has always been a constant theme in my life. Ever since I was a little kid, I would imagine the worst-case scenario. In the area I grew up in, there was a big difference between a "Fight" and "War." Most teenagers in middle school and high school remember getting into "a Fight," which meant that for whatever reason, they exchanged punches or kicks or hair-pulling with somebody they didn't like or didn't like them, and somebody either "won" or "lost." After the "fight" was over "it was done." It just becomes a "back-in-the-day" story of, "I fought him or her in eighth grade" or "I fought him or her in tenth grade." And that's it, that's the full story. Done.

Well, this was not <u>my</u> reality. One-on-one "Fights" existed, but only if arranged at someone's request, to squash a personal beef. My reality was called "War." "War" in the East Side meant that if you "crossed me/disrespected me/or wanted some" with me, "it was on"—War was declared. From that point forward, you now became my permanent enemy. And it didn't matter who "won" the 1st time or the last time, because with "War," the new rule was to, "Attack On Sight!"—every single time. In "War," it was no longer about a "one-on-one fight," instead it was mutually understood that, "Every time I see you; every time any of my friends see you—the chase is on" from now, until forever. This type of "War" also includes targeting your family's home, cars and little brothers and sisters as well, as long as they are "of age" to withstand a beating.

For example, one day, around 6 pm, as the sun was setting, seven of us friends between the ages of fourteen and seventeen decided to walk to the corner gas station on King Road, next door to Lee's Burgers. One of our solid homeboy wanted to buy some *"frajos."* Seven of us stood around the gas station's parking lot waiting. After purchasing the pack of cigarettes, we started walking back to the "kick-it spot." Well, on our way back, we spot a fine-looking hyna walking down King Road towards the 680 overpass. Well, my older brother and my best-friend's older brother—both decide to whistle at her to get her attention. She decided to stop—so my brother Droopy and Diablo started walking towards her. The rest of us youngsters waited for them while they got their "mack on."

As they are got closer to their destination, a guy around

their age, walked past them in the opposite direction on King Road, walking towards Story Road. Without hesitation, "On Sight," both my brother Droopy and Diablo did a 180 and began to chase him. Because in "War"—my homeboys' enemies are now my enemies; hence, the other five of us standing nearby began chasing this vato as well at full speed, within 1.5 seconds of seeing the chase without asking why or who it was.

The guy sprinted like a lightning bolt into Lee's Burgers and began to yell, "Call the cops! Call the cops!"

One of the workers ran to the door, shut it, and locked the doors behind him. He got away "that time." But the reverse story also plays true. I've made many "U-turns" while walking and had to sprint to get away "those times" also. This is why I continue to try to avoiding confrontations now as an adult, because I know a never-ending war can result. I would hate to waste another decade of my life worrying about fools creeping.

The older woman and I continued to walk up Bowers Ave northbound, passing Central Expressway, then over the crossing over the 101 freeway where the street changed names again into Great America Parkway. The older woman continued walking quickly and I wondered why is she walking so fast? Why is she in such a hurry? Then I noticed the older woman cross the street to the left side and entered into her destination—the Our Lady of Peace Church, where the big metallic statue stands. I didn't understand why this woman walked over an hour, in the cold darkness, risking her safety, and sacrificing of sleep, to make it to early-morning mass?

I continued walking northbound. By this time, an hour and fifteen minutes later, the East Side sun finally rose behind me and its loving light warmed my entire back and shoulders. I was on the "home stretch," since 3COM Corporation was located at the intersection of Great America Parkway and the 287 Freeway. I reached my job-site destination one hour and a half after first leaving my bedroom near El Camino Real and Kiely Ave.

"You must not lose faith in humanity. Humanity is an ocean, if a few drops of the ocean are dirty, the ocean does not become dirty." —Mahatma Gandhi

"I might not have much, but I also lack nothing."

CHAPTER III

HIV TEST

I finally decided to grow a pair, and get tested. Waiting for those test results was the most frightening experience I'd ever went through, because I was facing a high probability of mortality at twenty years old, since I never used protection. I remember walking into the medical office, and waiting for the doctor to deliver the news to me. He told me I was "HIV negative." I was so relieved! Whew! But then the doctor kept a serious look on his face, and gave me a reality check. He explained to me that this HIV test was not 100% accurate because the HIV can actually "hide" in your body for about nine months without being detected. After asking the doctor several questions, I learned that the only way to know for sure that the HIV was not hiding in my body was to be 100% abstinent/celibate. This would be the biggest challenge of my life, but I needed to know for sure. During those long twelve months, I made a promise to My Mentor, "If you allow me to live, I will no longer live for me, but I will dedicate the rest of my life to serve anybody and everybody you place in front of me."

A year later, the doctor handed me the results of the second test. I took a deep breath, silently asked my Mentor again for mercy and I opened the envelope. The moment I finished reading the words, "HIV—Negative"—I died. The original life I was given at birth—which I ruined with my selfishness was gone. From that day on—I was re-born.

"Be careful with your thoughts, they become words.
Be careful with your words, they become actions.
Be careful with your actions, they become habits.
Be careful with your habits, they become your reputation.
Be careful with your reputation, it becomes your values.
And Be careful with your values, it becomes your Destiny." - Frank Outlaw

ANGELS IN DISGUISE

About half ways through my 2nd year in college, I was with a girlfriend that I "fell in love" with, and she cared enough to notice that all my grades had dropped to mostly C's with a couple of F's. This new girlfriend asked me why I was jeopardizing my tuition-free education at Santa Clara University? Other random people also began to ask me the same question, so I began to think about an answer.

I was at a crossroads-dilemma. I thought about it and thought about it for several weeks—trying to decide between holding on to my past life; or taking a risk and strive to achieve all my dreams towards an unknown future? I knew it was the two people inside of me, "Silent vs. Enrique," that were pulling me in two very different directions. I knew that I had to decide to either hang out 100% with my homeboys and disregard my studies, or put 100% effort into school and become a serious student? Since, it was now impossible to try to "play both sides of the fence." With sadness, I decided to "fly solo" once again. I decided to no longer check my mail box and "disappear into the shadows" again.

Slowly but surely, my grades began to climb up again. But deep down inside, I stopped caring about school. I stopped studying for tests/exams. I felt like I had died inside. My chest on the inside felt hollow, cold, and empty. I stopped calling my parents for 2-3 weeks at a time. I would randomly break up with girlfriends by changing my pager number without telling them. I stayed distracted with random sexual encounters and continued to "represent" and "hit people up" even though my friends weren't around. I remember laying on my bed one day, in my dorm room, with the door open, blasting my oldies music full volume, not giving a fuck. Suddenly, someone shows up at my doorway. It was a Black guy in his early 30's. My first response was to look at him in his eye and sternly ask, "Wutz'up?" He went into his automatic long speech, trying to sell me something. I wasn't interested, so I said, "Naw, maybe next time."

"*Everybody is a Teacher — If you Listen*" — Doris Roberts

At that exact moment, time stood still, the air changed in the room, and my loud music faded into the distance. This young man looked at me with a serious, but sincere look in his eyes, and proceeded to utter seven words that caught my attention and that I have never forgotten since that day, ten years later. This stranger delivered a message to my soul. With complete confidence, he said to me, "You know you've gotta stay here right?" He must have seen that I didn't want to be there anymore. Maybe he read my body language or maybe he simply obeyed his intuition. I looked at him confused and said, "Huh?" And he repeated himself, "You know you gotta stay here." I remained on my bed, in silence, but this time I was listening attentively. He disregarded his sales pitch and in "real talk" stated, "There's not that many people like us in places like these." And at that point I knew exactly what he was saying. He knew nobody could relate to me here. He somehow already knew I felt isolated here. He knew that I felt incarcerated in my little dorm room far away from my real home.

I sat up, shook his hand, and introduced myself. I told him I didn't have any money to buy anything off of him, but to come back tomorrow for sure. I appreciated his words of encouragement, which awoke me from my slumber. The next day I waited for him to return. The messenger never came back. Maybe it was because it was against the rules for off-campus vendors to solicit. That man might never know this, but he helped me stay at SCU, while I was home-sick and "done" with school.

"People enter into our lives for a Reason, a Season, or a Lifetime." —Anonymous

"As an educated Latino —I have now become HIS-Panic."

FROM ESSJ TO SCU AND BACK

My co-workers would often notice dozens of my "girlfriends" come by the job site, on a daily basis, to bring me lunch or to visit. My co-workers didn't understand how a guy could be so "successful" with females. I loved this admiration, because it helped boost my self-esteem. One day, a co-worker said to me, "Wow, you should write a book!" In other words, what he was saying is that I should write a book to teach the "Average Joe" how to pick up on females. I thought it was a funny statement, but it planted the first book idea in my head.

I wanted my book to serve a greater purpose, so I had the idea of using my book to give a voice to those in prison who endure injustices and human rights violations. I received a lot of testimonials from prison. However, I began to doubt this idea because I asked myself, "Who am I for the government and voters to listen to and make changes?" So I gave up and abandoned the book idea. About six months later, my mentor gave me idea to write something that would help other "Pony Boys" like me other there, still searching for guidance.

As I wrote and vented my painful memories, I felt better. It was my self-administered therapy, letting it all out. My first book, entitled, From E.S.S.J., to S.C.U., and Back, helped me to heal and described the evolution of my mind. Now, it serves as an intervention and prevention workbook for teens to write in, to create their book, their story. Friends convinced me to try to publish it. So, I took the chance and I sent thirty copies of the book to thirty publishers; and, two months later, I received thirty rejection letters. I gave up trying.

The cover of the first book is of me squatting down in front of the image of La Virgen de Guadalupe. One of the most painful comments I've ever heard, was from a mom in my community, who told her daughter that *"Es una desgracia que ese cholo este junto a La Virgen de Guadalupe."* This truly hurt my feelings.

I got tired such negative stereotypes, so I shaved off my mustache, I let the hair on my head grow out, I bought and began wearing button up dress shirts and tucked them into my pants, I bought butt-hugger slacks, I bought shiny dress shoes, but to no avail. People still told me I looked liked a cholo. I was so confused. I gave up trying and just dressed however I felt comfortable. I thought to myself, if I can't change my looks, I'll change my life style. So, I chose to modify my mind, dress, and actions into a new age "cholo-scholar hybrid" model.

"Don't judge a book by its' cover, nor the by the 1st chapter; even if the chapter is ten years long" —Father G-Dog

OMENS

For 2-3 consecutive months, an unusual and eerie phenomenon was occurring. People from my past that I had either avoided or had unresolved issues with because crossing paths with me. Almost like a speedy reunion.

On several occasions, a fog of terror would float by pass by, causing an overwhelming feeling of terror that would affect even those standing around me.

While talking outside La Casa Azteca Mex Restaurant with a female friend. I saw a white owl in the sky, flying towards my direction, I followed its flight my eyes glued to its movements. At it got directly over my head, it abruptly changed directions dramatically, at a forty-five degree angle towards the east hills.

My friend looked at me and said, "Did you see that? Why did it do that? I've never seen a white owl before. That's not a good sign?" It's almost as if its' only purpose was just to deliver its' message to me.

According to the movie, *"Mi Familia"* and Mexican folklore—a white owl represents a warning of death approaching.

This white owl reminded me that I was living on "borrowed time." In other words, the omen was clear, "don't bother making plans" because the angel of death is on its way.

Great Mentor, "...grant me the serenity [and maturity] to accept the things I cannot change; the courage to change the things I can; and the wisdom to know the difference." - Reinhold Niebuhr

SLY, SLICK, AND WICKED

I was working in the game-room, as usual playing pool, foosball, and ping-pong with the youngsters; when suddenly, two female co-workers sprint inside yelling over and over again.

"Call the cops!," "Call the police!"

I ask in a concerned voice, "What happened?"

They replied almost in unison, "There's a fight in the front!"

Since I was still a rookie in the field, my 1st response was to find my supervisor or a co-worker who was more experienced than I was in handling such a situation. I urgently looked inside all the offices, but saw nobody. As I was walking back to the front desk, prepared to do my duty, I ran into one of my male co-workers and informed him.

"The girls said there's a fight out front."

My coworker asks, "Is it one of our kids?"

I replied, "They weren't sure"

So, we both proceeded to run out front to make sure our kids were okay.

As we ran along the side of the building, we see two gang members sprint across the parking lot, jump over a fence, and start getting into their car. I keep running straight forward towards my destination to see if any kids were hurt. My co-worker decided to make a right turn towards the two older dudes, and jumped over the same fence, attempting to stop them from fleeing.

I finally get to the front of the building and see three teens standing at the bus stop. They seemed calm and uninjured. I then decided to go back and back up my coworker as I was trained by veteran staff. As I turn the corner, I see my coworker standing outside the car window - still trying to convince the two guys not to flee the scene, pleading with them loudly, "Wait!" "Wait!" As I'm walking towards them, I decided to assist my coworker by writing down the license plate number. As I'm writing down the plates, the driver looks back at that exact moment and scans me from head to toe.

After we go back to work, I felt proud of myself. Being new to this service-field, I put into action a lot of my training. Namely, a. Working as a team and backing up coworkers in any situation; b. Under the "Mandated Reporting Law," meant that I had to put the safety of our teens as the top priority, above all else. I liked my job and I wanted to do a good job. The next day, I noticed a "missed call" from my boss. I thought she was going to give me props for my quick-response to the situation, working as a team, and reporting everything I saw — since a couple of weeks before I had gotten in trouble at work for not reporting something a teen told me "in confidence."

When I finally checked my voicemail, I heard a message from my supervisor stating, "Don't come into work today." Confused, I called her back and asked "Why?" All she said was, "Please meet us at the main office. We need to talk to you about something." Now, I was getting frustrated because it seemed like I could NEVER do anything right at my new job!

I walked into the conference room and saw my three supervisors. They proceeded to tell me that I couldn't go back to work at the youth center because it was not safe for me. They said that twelve older gang members from that neighborhood had come to the teen-center looking for me. This news surprised me, and I immediately got defensive and asked, "Three other co-workers responded to the same situation. Why am I being singled-out?" I broke-it-down to my supervisors, explaining play-by-play, how the entire incident yesterday was a team-response. Two female coworkers saw the fight, ran in, they called the police. I looked for my supervisors. When I didn't find any, a male coworker and I both ran outside to check on the safety of our kids. The male coworker tried stopping the fleeing vehicle and I wrote down the license plate. Four employees were involved in that response and I was the only one sitting in this meeting. I felt I got "thrown under the bus." One of my supervisors, who is also the gang intervention specialist confirmed my thoughts, by stating that it was evident to him that the gang never liked me working in their neighborhood from the beginning, since in their eyes, I was a rival - so, they were waiting for any excuse to get rid of me.

I told my supervisors that I didn't want to put any kids in danger, so for that reason only, I would not go back. Before leaving, I went into the restroom to pee. As I was washing my hands, a "coworker" whom had known ties to the neighborhood-gang, and had never spoken to me before, started acting "friendly" towards me.

He asked, "So...what gang did you used to kick it with?"

In my street-wise mind, I knew exactly what was going on. This undercover was trying to do his "homework" on me, trying to figure out how much back-up I had. So, I gave him my usual answer.

"Yeah, I grew up around Story & King."

Leaving the rest for him and his gang to fill in the blanks however they wanted.

I was sad leaving, because I liked my job working with at-risk teens. Every six months, the youth-center would call me and invite me back to work, because they said the threat was over and the kids were asking about me. But I followed my gut-instinct, and never accepted the invitations because I didn't trust the "inside informant" who still worked there.

About four years later, the youth center called me again and invited me to attend their annual Role-Model Conference. I accepted. When I got there, I "scope everything out." The gang-intervention friend of mine welcomed me and told me "Sit down bro, grab some food pointing at the buffet tables in the back I said, "thanks," but, I instead decide to grab a folding chair from one of the round tables and remove myself from the crowd, by sitting alone in the very back. The spot I decided to sit at, I had the youth center behind me, the buffet tables were to my left and the round tables and stage was in front of me. On purpose I sat next to an iron beam to the right side of my head, so that nobody could see me as they walked up. I positioned myself in that spot on purpose because it was not in the path of any foot-traffic and all entrances were within my view at all times.

As I sat there—I scanned every single person from head-to-toe. Immediately, I noticed "the inside leak" ex-coworker sitting at one of the round-tables with his family. He had not noticed me yet. All was peaceful. Everybody was either, standing at the buffet line to my left, sitting, eating and watching the entertainment in front of me, or playing in the youth center behind me. Every person's body movements were flowing naturally according to the event. Suddenly, the "air atmosphere-changed." I noticed the moment "the wolf in sheep's clothing" turned around naturally, but his head paused in surprise as he spotted me. At this point, everything became slow-motion. I knew exactly what would happen next, because my "street-smarts" helps me predict behavior. Being "street-smart" means being able to see early warning signs before it happens, and then avoiding that trouble.

If you were sitting right next to me at that very moment, I would have leaned over and whispered to you,

"Watch… He's not going to look back at me anymore, but in about 20-30 seconds, he's going to lean over to tell his wife he needs to go to the restroom. Yep, that's exactly what he did. Now, watch how awkwardly he walks up the steps in front of us, because now he's trying to be natural. He now has to pretend he's not in a hurry, so he's going to walk extra slow. See! Look at that! Now, he's going to be in there about 10-15 seconds to make "the phone call," and stall about thirty additional seconds, to make believe he went to go pee. He walks back calmly without looking in my direction at all. Ok, now that he made the phone call to his neighborhood gang. In about one-to-five minutes, at least 10-15 fools are going to walk up to this center and block off all exits. Given that prediction, I now have one to four minutes to decide, Cut-out and bounce, or face the hurricane storm approaching.

My logic common-sense told me to leave immediately! But for some odd reason, I felt no fear. Instead my body felt confidently calm. The only reason I was there was because I was invited to serve as a "role model" for the teens of that neighborhood. I sat there, away from the crowd and waited. All body movements were again flowing naturally. Kids were walking in and out of the youth center to my right-hand side, families were still getting "seconds" at the buffet table to my left side, and families were still sitting, talking, and enjoying the entertainment on stage in front of me. Four minutes went by, and I sat there, still expecting 10-15 neighborhood gang members to run up and pull the rush move they have been itching for. At five minutes past the initial "phone call" was made, something unexpected caught my attention. My peripheral vision, to my left-side, noticed an <u>abnormal</u> body movement, walking towards my direction. I turned my head to my left to gather more data, and I saw a skinny teenage girl, about fifteen years of age, dressed in *"cholita"* attire, with a determined demeanor. It was a sunny and warm day out, so it was strange that this teenage girl was wearing a hooded-sweater with the hood over her head and zipped up to the top with both her hands inside her sweater pockets. I turned my head away towards the main stage again, confused, but still alert and aware of her and everybody's body movements.

I re-assessed the scene quickly using my logic to try to make sense of why this teenage girl arrived late to this event, and walking in my direction? Maybe she was hungry? Nope, she walked right past the four buffet tables without even glancing at the delicious food items Maybe she knew somebody attending this large event? Nope, she didn't look at any of the round tables where people were sitting. Maybe she wanted to enjoy the entertainment on stage? Nope, she didn't even notice the people dancing on the stage. Maybe she's heading to the game room inside the youth center? Yeah, I'm **sure** that's it. Fully expecting her to walk by in front of me then make a right turn into the youth center, like all the other teens.

As I continued watching her every step, from the corner of my left eye, my suspicion grows. Because instead of walking in front of me, like all the others, she angled abruptly to walk behind me. Since she walked behind my peripheral vision, disappearing out of sight I turned my head to the left side immediately to make sure she proceeded into the youth center, since that was the only logical option remaining to explain such a *"movida."*

To recap, this skinny girl, around fifteen years old, wearing a light grey hooded sweatshirt, with both hands in her sweater-pockets, walked passed up the food, past the tables with guests, past the entertainment stage, and instead of going past me, into the teen center, she decides to STOP BEHIND ME! She stops walking, turns her body, and stands behind my chair, while I'm still sitting there!. At this point, my "Spider-Sense" goes off! And within 0.5 seconds, I get up from my chair, pivot to my left, to turn around completely, and I'm now facing her three steps away.

What happens next stuns me as her intentions become crystal clear. When I got up from the chair in haste and turned around to face her, it was obvious that she wasn't expecting that reaction from me. Why? Because she froze for five seconds, as she looked down at my empty chair. During those five seconds, I noticed her left hand was out of her pocket, down by her side but her right hand was still inside her sweater's pocket holding on to something. This object which created a bulge inside her pocket, was pointing directly behind my chair, at the level where the back of my head was five seconds ago.

I stood there in a defensive stance, ready to respond to this "curve ball." But in my heart, mind, and soul felt deeply sad and confused. I couldn't believe this was happening. Her next move, confirmed my suspicion to 100% certainty. After those five long seconds, she got an, "Oh crap" look on her face, so she immediately rotated her entire body to the right, to hide the bulge in her right side pocket. But, now in this panic-mode, she failed to realize that she now was facing a blue-colored iron beam twelve inches WIDE. So, now she felt even more stupid, because she stood there **again** frozen for five more second facing this blue iron beam, two inches away from her nose!

At this point, my mind was racing - trying to decide what to do next as I observed all of this in front of me. Should I get the attention of the gang intervention staff person walking by towards the teen center at that moment? Or should I reach out and grab the object in her right hand?; which she was still holding on to inside her sweater pocket this entire time. But what would people think, say, or do if they saw me grab this teenage girl? Or, should I keep looking at her to see what she does next? Well, by the time I finished considering these three options, the intervention staff person walked by into the youth center. This girl decided to "play it off cool," rotated her body again, and walked into the front door of the youth center.

I must have been in shock, because I stood there transfixed, looking at the front doors of the center. I've never encountered an incident like this, so I just waited. Twenty seconds later the same girl walked out, now with both her hands out and walked past me, the same direction she walked in, passing up the delicious food again, and disappeared back into her gang neighborhood.

For some odd reason, I decided to stay and fulfill my obligation. The next twenty minutes I sat there, on the same chair, perplexed - trying to figure out if I truly just experienced what I believe I just experienced. I tried in earnest to figure out a logical answer to the question, "Why did she come here? If she didn't eat, didn't sit, didn't talk to anybody, and didn't play inside the youth center?." I "never saw it coming" because I would have never suspected a teenage girl to serve the role of a "hit man."

I was in a daze for the rest of the role-model conference.

MY RETURN TO LEE MATHSON

"It happened here." I pointed to the green grass outside the chain-linked fence entrance. I had not been back here to Lee Mathson Middle School, in eight years. However, nobody knew that my mind traveled to this very spot every single day. My world changed forever after that unforgettable day. Before that day, I believed in street rules, in the old street "code." That "old code" of respect meant that if you saw an enemy walking with his mom, sister, girlfriend, or any little kid—you let him slide. The old code of respect meant that if you and five comrades approached an enemy caught slippin by himself, you would ask him, "Who do you want to box/knuckle up with?" That old code taught me that only fair-fights count. That you couldn't brag about "winning" a fight if you had an unfair advantage by size, weapon, numbers, or blind-sided someone with a sucker-punch.

That day, in eighth grade, while laying on my back, losing this fair-fight, I saw a twelve-inch screwdriver sticking out of his back pocket. But I didn't grab it because it would not be fair to do so. He didn't believe in the same old-code that I did, because he grabbed it and "stuck" me with that cold metal tip three times. He believed in the philosophy of, "Win by any means necessary. And after you win, add insult to injury."

After the stabbing occurred, I walked to a comrade's house across the street. I walked to his restroom to look at my injuries in the mirror. I did not recognize my face. The left side of my nose was swollen. I also noticed dried blood on the edges of my nostrils. The inside of my left eye-socket ached with pain. I took off my shirt and noticed one slash cut on my left bicep and two flat head screwdriver holes on top of my right shoulder.

When my comrade walked into the restroom to check on me, I made my first request, "Do you have peroxide?" He said yeah, and reached under the sink. I leaned my right shoulder over the sink and told him to pour the peroxide on top of the open wounds. I placed two band-aids over the two holes that penetrated my flesh. Then I spoke my second request, "Where's your phone?" After trying several phone numbers with no answer, I made my third and final request, "Give me a knife." My comrade went to his kitchen, got a five-inch kitchen knife, and handed it to me. I grabbed the kitchen knife, walked back outside, and I picked it up a broken broom stick I saw on the ground on my way out. About eight minutes had passed since the initial stabbing occurred. I walked with a determined pace down Sinclair street towards the Mayfair Community Center, carrying half a broom stick in my left hand and a kitchen knife in my right hand.

I was now in tunnel-vision mode. I didn't care if the police were in the area or if anybody on the public street noticed the weapons in my hands. I walked through the front door of the Mayfair Center and scanned the room from left to right - searching for my target. The youngsters inside immediately backed-up away from me. I checked every single room in the youth center, even the back patio outside—but he was nowhere in sight. I walked back out the front entrance and proceeded to my second search area—"Mayfair Park," behind the Our Lady of Guadalupe Church. I walked behind the Mayfair Center, but he wasn't there either; so, without losing pace, I walked towards my third search area—Cesar Chavez Elementary School. A homeboy who had heard what had happened, drove around looking for me until he spotted me walking down Kammerer Ave and told me to get in the car.

We drove back to my neighborhood - to the kickback house. I walked into the house and saw eight homeboys sitting in the living room. They all got up and asked me what happened? I told them. Their automatic response was, "Let's go." So we all walked outside to get into the white civic. However, only half of us got into the car, because a debate had ensued, It wasn't clear if a war had been declared between the two homeboy gangs? Or if this was a personal beef between a few? So, it was decided that it would remain a personal beef. I walked home to put ice on my nose to get the swelling down and get dressed. My eighth grade graduation ceremony was going to begin in two hours at Independence High School. My dad left work early, because he was looking forward to watching his boy graduate from middle school like all the other proud parents.

After that dark day, I carried my knife every single day. I decided not to seek revenge. Instead, I decided to "play defense" not offense. In the mean time, I decided to get physically stronger and wait patiently for "Round two," whenever the universe decided to cross our paths again at the destined time and place. For eight years I stayed ready. For eight years I thought of nothing else. For eight years I prepared and ate hate for breakfast, lunch, and dinner. But My Mentor had other plans for me....

A friend of mine mailed me a copy of Brother Ig's CD Album *"Off the Crooked Path."* The following lyrics describes the conversation I had with My Mentor,

Me

"...I know you're with me, but sometimes I feel all alone.
I'm here with people I don't know!

My Mentor

I will raise you into a leader. Just keep your eyes on me.
Your loved ones will then follow, you just wait and see.
Believe in me and let me change your heart.
My light will shine through you for those in the dark.

Me

But what about my boys? I left them in the battlefield!

My Mentor

Well, I called you to another battle; so pick up your shield and your sword.

Head out to war and win those lost souls...."

Today I returned to Lee Mathson to face the scene of the crime. But what brought me here was not a thirst for revenge nor a desire to heal from that trauma; instead, I arrived at Lee Mathson because I had good news to share. I had the power to provide Lee Mathson students other young "Silents" with "a chance of a life time"—namely, free admission into Bellarmine with a full ride that included, free tuition, free books, free lunch, and free bus passes.

The first day of my outreach work, I spent the entire day there at Lee Mathson talking to all the Boys, trying to convince them to leave all their friends behind, go to an all-boy school, and do 3-5 hours of homework every night? Of course they all said, "Heck No!" So, I decided to stop doing classroom presentations. Instead I just hung out during lunch, supervising the lunch time detention, always full. The vice-principal noticed that I got along well with the students so she asked me if I would be interested in running a group after school. I said yes and volunteered my time, three days after school, for six months.

After our "Deep Circle" groups ended, I would continue to mentor the way my school counselor Rob mentored me.

"Every tree is known by its fruit."—Luke 6,44

"The best way to destroy an enemy—is to make them a friend."—Abraham Lincoln

"Life can only be understood backwards; but it must be lived forward." — *Soren Kierkegaard*

"The best inheritance you can leave your children, is a good quality education." — *Ventura Zúñiga*

"Let your passion, light your path." — *Father Tom Allender, S.J.*

CHAPTER IV.

HALF MOON BAY

It was a sunny morning in San Jose the first time I decided to drive to Half-Moon Bay by myself. I had my map quest "drawing" next to me as I drove on the 101 freeway. As I got near the 95 freeway off ramp, I began to feel nervous. Why? Because the sunny blue sky soon disappeared. Looking out my window to my left, I saw something I had never seen in my life. A wall of dark fog rolled over the mountain tops like an army, charging down the side of the mountains towards me.

I immediately realized that the powers of darkness were trying to prevent me from getting to my destination. I was on a quest to see and speak with my Mentor. It was an unannounced visit. You see, I wandered away too far, and now was lost, unable to find my way back "home." So, I decided to go seek to be found. I arrived at the beach and it was empty. The ocean waves that wiped away clean all the previous footprints from the sand. It looked and felt like I was the first person ever to walk on this beach.

I had arrived at this wide-open space, by the ocean's edge to be easily be spotted by my mentor whenever He glanced in this direction. I was determined to be found this day, so I unloaded a fold up beach chair I bought at the store, I unloaded some peaches I had packed to snack on, and I unloaded two plastic bottles of orange juice to drink when I got thirsty. I sat there, on my beach chair, enjoying the cool breeze traveling from across the Pacific Ocean. I sat there, writing in my journal, thinking and reflecting in gratitude for my life.

"*That evening,*

I fell into a deep sleep.

I dreamt I was walking along this beach with his Mentor.

As I walked, I looked up at the blue sky above me, and I recognized memories I had experienced during my life.

Each memory flashed one at a time, like a huge slide show up in the sky.

The memories looked so vivid and real, that the sky became like the giant IMAX movie theatre screen dome.

As I continued walking down the beach, near the edge of the shore, I continued looking up at the sky, and re-lived those experiences like an emotional roller-coaster.

After several minutes passed, I turned around to see how far I had walked, and I noticed footsteps pressed into the sand.

A wave of sadness crashed over my body, feeling a deep loneliness.

I noticed that in the beginning of our walk, two sets of footprints were pressed into the sand. One belonging to me and the other belonging to my Mentor.

But as I followed the path of my footsteps with my eyes, I noticed that about half ways along the beach, only one set of footprints remained.

I felt like I was standing there alone, lost, rejected, and abandoned, especially during the most painful moments of my life.

Feeling hurt, I asked my Mentor in disappointment,

"Mentor, you promised that if I did everything you said, you would be with me the entire way. Why did your footprints disappear when I needed you most!?"

My Mentor stood beside me in silence.

My Mentor then faced me, reached out with His right hand, gently holding my shoulder and calmly said,

"My precious, precious child,

I love you

and I told you I would never leave you.

I have been with you every single day of your life. You must believe that the sun still exists, even when it is night time. In the same way, believe that I am here always, even when I am invisible.

The truth is, during those times of loneliness, stress, pain, and loss, when you felt you suffered alone,

it was then that I carried you."

- Author Unknown

On June 18th 6-18, I stood at edge of the ocean, facing it, asking my mentor,
"Divine Mentor, here I am. I don't have much. Here I am, with my hands and my pockets empty.

What if this is it? What if this is everything I will ever accomplish? Will you accept me as I am?"
It was evening time on 6-18, when I walked down the sand to the sea. It had already grown dark, and the sun slowly set behind the blanket of ocean. But my mentor had not yet appeared, so I waited, I deeply wished to hear my mentor's voice and feel the emptiness in my chest fill with warmth, love, and peace. The sea was rough due to the strong wind blowing. The waves crashing towards me. Suddenly I saw my mentor, disguised as a dark brown seal, arrive at the edge of the shore.
At 6,18 pm, my mentor said, "It is me, do not be afraid. You are free now. Today, 6-18, at 6,18 pm - I will make a pact with you. I will do my part, but please do your part. Do what is right and good in my sight. I will await for you to return."

EAST SIDE HEROES

"The worst thing in the world—is wasted talent." —"A Bronx Tale" movie.

I'm a dreamer. I dream every single night, and when I'm awake, I continue to "day dream." My Mentor blessed me with a vivid imagination - with the ability to see beyond the obvious. As a little kid, I used to look at the brown wood patterns on the wall paper and be able to see faces or animal figures. When I got older, as a teenager, I would look outside my apartment window and I would see the abandoned warehouse next to King's Super. I would day dream about winning the lottery, buying that building and building a youth center there for East Side kids.

"The man who moves a mountain begins by carrying away small stones." —*Confucius*

Sometimes these visions were planted by other people, since my friends and many mentors "Believed in me before I believed in myself." A Jesuit priest Padre Luis Calero once told me during my 2nd year of college, "I see you doing talks like Father Boyle one day." My first initial thought reaction was, "Yeah right! I hate talking in front of people." So, I explained to Fr. Calero, "I'm always the tree in class skits." A few months later, I agreed to do my first talk ever at "Washington Youth Center." I was super nervous, so I sat for two hours the night before to prepare and write a speech. The next day, I stood in front of a room of teens and I began to read the speech I had written the night before. I was too intimidated to look directly into the eyes of my audience; so, I had to look up to the ceiling or the side wall or down at the ground. I began stuttering bad, trying to read my messy hand-writing. I noticed the kids were bored out of their mind, and some got up and left! I got even more embarrassed and my forehead began to drip with sweat! I was convinced with 100% sureness that I wasn't good at public speaking. So I stopped doing talks for a long time.

I felt directionless. After watching the movie, "Motorcycle Diaries," I began to seriously consider living outside my comfort-zone. I was ready and open to go where ever My Mentor wanted me to go. I applied for jobs in San Francisco, up the Peninsula, Santa Cruz, etc. I even got a job offer response from a job in Compton! So I began imagining myself moving down to the LA area; but I stayed open to signs.

"Humbleness must be achieved before Promotion."

Soon after, I received the news, "Father Boyle has cancer." I knew i had to go down to L.A. to see him—My intuition said so. While on the airplane, I read and reflected on the story of Martha and Mary. Martha was the workaholic, serving others 24-7. Mary chose to be still and enjoy peacefulness. The lesson was loud and clear, "There is only one thing that is important, and Mary chose the better half with the Good Mentor. The parable stated that only one thing is expected, and "the better half" is enjoying peace next to the Great Mentor, over serving others. So I learned to no longer feel guilty for resting and taking days off, even if others need at the same time.

Before I flew down to LA, I wrote my will and made peace with My Mentor at Half-Moon Bay. I was ready to die. After talking to Father G about my experience on the plane and arriving to see him, he said, "Sounds like the spell is finally broken." While waiting at the LAX airport, I went into a bookstore to browse, and discovered the book, "Just Give Me Chuy." I read it for hours and hours non-stop. While in the sky on the airplane ride back home, I died a second time. I surrendered to my Mentor's Plan, not my own. When the airplane landed, I knew I had been granted "Round two." You see, I never imagined my life past 30 years old. I never thought I'd live that long. But, when the plane landed, my commitment to start East Side Heroes' was born. I wasn't sure how long of an "extension" I was granted; but, I did know that I was now living on "borrowed time."

From the San Jose Airport, I got a taxi to my Bellarmine office, and I went straight to my computer. I sat down on my chair and typed a short email message to everybody I knew. I told people, "I am now ready to create my 'Master Piece' or in other words, "My Master's Peace." On my drive home, I called three of my closest East Sider friends Ruben, Gabriel, Alberto, and I invited them to an important lunch meeting at Red Robin Restaurant at Eastridge Mall. The next day, I spent the entire day typing out the East Side Heroes' Mission Statement and a three-year Vision Plan of this new nonprofit idea of mine. I explained to them that I knew this was not a "team effort" in creating the Mission Statement and Vision Plan from scratch, but I would truly be honored if they would join my team. From that lunch meeting on, East Side Heroes was launched. We started strategically planning our first event.

Miraculously, it wasn't until a few nights later, that I realized that I had no more nightmares of ghosts. Even more miraculous, I was no longer had any fear of the dark. Father G was right—"The curse WAS finally broken." I went full-speed forward with my new East Side Heroes' nonprofit. I was fearless and super optimistic. I was no longer intimidated by any TV interview, or radio interview, or newspaper interview. No politicians, chief of police, or CEO intimidated me either. The mountain of obstacles, complications, and odds stacked against me did not slow me down nor cause me any stress. I announced the date of the event and selected a scholarship recipient, way before any donation checks came in. My mentor was by my side. It was His idea actually, so I KNEW it couldn't fail. I had been entrusted a new mission to my destiny, so I knew I would be kept safe until I completed my assignment.

It was like knowing you only have ten seconds remaining in a heavy weight championship boxing match. If this is the last round of your life—what would you do? Inside my heart and soul, I heard "my coach" slap the canvas twice as hard as He could -*THUMP! THUMP!*; to get my attention -*THUMP! THUMP!*; to unleash my inner jaguar -*THUMP! THUMP!*; to focus only on His voice and His instructions -*"THUMP! THUMP!*; to let me know "There are only 10 SECONDS LEFT!, No more time for wasting. Go all out! It's now or never.

Launch that "Hail Mary Pass." My Mentor was giving me "one last round," and I had to give it my all, my 100% effort at every moment, every second that is available to me.

"If not you—who? If not now—When?."—John F. Kennedy

One night, I received a spiritual email. This message was received via a vivid dream about East Side Heroes. In this dream, I was shown words, in a paragraph, but written backwards, as if though I had to be sitting on the other side of the page, looking in my direction, reading the words starting from the bottom left side of the page, and reading up, from left to right, like this,

…reverof tsal lliw dna rehto on

ekil nigeb lliw seoreH ediS tsaE

I don't remember what the entire paragraph said, but it was definitely about East Side Heroes. I dream every single night, so when I get these type of dreams, I pay extra attention, because everything in the dream is crystal clear and out of the ordinary. For instance, in another night dream, I dreamt my wife and I were walking through a garden during the night and we saw a large and round Aztec Calendar standing in the center of this garden.

"Luck = is when Preparation meets Opportunity."— Seneca

As my wife and I walked past the garden and got on board a city bus, I heard a voice that said out-loud, "Go where the heart is, the place with heart." This dream was very weird. When I awoke in the morning, I knew immediately this was one of those "spiritual email." So, I went to the store to purchase some paint and I decided to paint the Aztec calendar that I remember seeing. It took me a few weeks to complete it, but I was determined not to forget the image. During those two weeks, I picked up the Metro Horoscope, and I was shocked at what I read under my sign, Sagittarius. The astrologist said that she was driving down a road, somewhere in the East Bay, when she heard an audible voice speak a phrase that she didn't understand. This psychic astrologist said that she heard the following words repeated out loud a couple of times, "Go where the heart is, the place with heart."

I was shocked. My 1st reaction was, "What da!??!?!?! What are the odds of this being a coincidence?" I still don't know what it means, but I'm positive the true meaning will be revealed to me at the right time.

Recently, I found some old letters from family, mentors, and even some from my old counselor. Here is one of those letters,

"Dear Enrique. It was so good to see you at the Mission Church a few weeks ago. You looked great, sounded good, and seemed happy. As you spoke, I was marveling at the growth I've witnessed in you.

When I first met you that day you visited Bellarmine as a Freshman, you seemed kind of cold and hard, difficult to talk to...

But when we talked last month, you seemed warm and friendly, comfortable with yourself and whom you're becoming and were much more generous with smiles.

I was impressed by your desire to serve people...You've always had a good heart, which I saw when you tutored students at Most Holy Trinity and men at the Day Worker Job Center. I was particularly moved by the care you had for the Day Workers, how you were so shy most of the time, but came alive as you stood in front of them to teach them—keep that in mind as you discern your future. Thanks for all of those good conversations all along the way.

Fr. Scott SantaRosa, S.J." - Jan. 8th, 1997 12th grade = 18 years old

Ten seconds left.

"Go hard or go home"—Tim Westwood
THUMP! THUMP!

CHAPTER V

FISHING IN DEEP WATERS

One year, I taught my "Deep Circle" classes at Menlo-Atherton High School, to serve the at-risk students from East Palo Alto. One day after school, one of the girls in my class asked if she could go to the bathroom? I said, "Sure." The entire class was full of life, learning, and laughter, until she walked back in. Her eyes both overflowing with tears told us something bad had happened. Everybody instantly became silent, then two seconds later, they all got up out of their seats and stood around her in a circle asking,

"¡Qué pasó!? What happened!? ¡Qué Pasa!? What!? What!? Please tell us!"—She then turned her head, looked directly at one of the boys and said to him, "There's an ambulance and police outside your house."

His instant response was, "Shit!" and asked his boy for a ride home. They both sprinted out of the class. Half of the class went with them and the other half of the students stayed with me in the class. The students who stayed with me couldn't concentrate. They all sat imagining the worst, trying to guess what happened and waited nervously for a phone call or text message to come in with new details. I ended class early, and drove five of my kids home as I usually did, to make sure they hot home safe.

The next day, we had program after school as usual, and I found out what happened. The boy's house got "shot-up" by rival gang members. Both his uncle and friend were shot during the drive-by shooting. His uncle was shot in the neck and his neighborhood friend was shot twice in both legs. But instead of being sad, my kids walked in with smiles on their face! The entire class walked in, gave me hugs and hand-shakes, in gratitude to me. I wasn't sure why, until the same girl who received the phone call the day before, got up, and spoke for the entire group, stating, "This 'Deep Circle Program saved our lives! You see, we ALWAYS hang out in front of his house after school—ALWAYS, every single day. EVERYBODY knows that. Especially our enemies. And we all would have FOR SURE been there, yesterday, kickin it and if it weren't for this Deep Circle class Enrique, we would have gotten shot too. And with a big smile on her face and sincerity in her eyes, she said, That's why we wanted to say 'Thank you Enrique! You're our Guardian Angel!'."

"The ultimate measure of a man is not where he stands in moments of comfort and convenience; but where he stands at times of challenge and controversy. The true neighbor will risk his position, his prestige, and even his own life for the welfare of others." —Dr. Martin Luther King Jr.

After the program, I drove the kids home.

I asked the fifteen year old boy, "How do you feel going home?"

He responded with a sad tone in his voice, "*Bien,* but they still leaving me gangster songs on my voicemail saying they gonna kill me."

I asked, "Can you family move away?" He said, "Naw, we can't afford to move right now."

I drove past his house, took him to eat at Togo's, and I started brainstorming a safety plan. I kept insisting, "Do you have any family anywhere else?"

He thought long and hard, "*Pues, tengo una tía,* but I don't know if I can go over there?"

I handed him my cell phone, and said, "Call her."

I get very direct when I get into "Problem-Solving Mode."

I knew I wouldn't be able to go home and hope that he would be alive the next day. I went to the restroom and when I got back to the table, he gave me her response.

"She said yeah, but not till tomorrow."

I then said, "Órale, give me the phone."

I started making my phone calls now. It was around 7 pm by then. I asked a friend if this boy could sleep there tonight? Because I needed to drive him to his aunt's house in another city first thing in the morning. She said she would call me back in ten minutes.

I explained to the boy, "You're going to have to drop out of high school, you're too far behind in credits, and you can't stay at your house, or you put everybody in danger."

He agreed, because he knew I was right, and he trusted me.

Once I got the ok from my friend, I told the boy, "Ok, we gotta go get your stuff."

With a nervous look on his face he said, "I don't' know what my mom's going to say?"

I told him, "I'll do the talking, don't worry."

It was about 8 pm when we got to his house. This action was of course a risk for me too, because he lived in a very violent neighborhood, inside a very violent city - especially given the fact that his house had just been shot-up by a dozen bullets the day before! And he was still receiving active death threats via phone because the original destination of the bullets were intended to enter his body. As I walked into his house, it was a very surreal sight. The first thing I noticed as I walked in, was three little children all under the age of ten, sitting on the living room floor watching TV, keeping their heads below the window sill. All the adults were standing alongside the two side walls, avoiding the open space in front of the windows as well. I spent an hour trying to convince his mom in Spanish that she needed to sell the house and move the family away to a safer area.

Some of the male family members made it known by their glares and grumbling that they were not happy with me being there inside their house because they felt that it was none of my business to offer any advice. But I was persistent, conveying an urgency in my voice, as I anticipated another drive-by shooting to occur at any moment. Common sense told me I shouldn't have been there, and that I should have left as soon as I felt the physical threats from the six men inside the house; but, I had already made up my mind that I was not going to leave without the safety of this boy I cared for.

I had to do everything in my power to try to save this young boy's life. He was only fifteen years old, who inherited this gang infested city. I explained to his mom that I had already arranged for him to stay at a friend's house for a couple of nights. I saw his mom—hesitating. So, I made a bold "executive decision" in the presence of his entire family. I told the boy, "Get your stuff, we gotta go." His mom didn't want her little boy leaving home, but she knew deep down inside that I was right. She knew that as long as he lived there, the younger kids and everybody else in that house was in grave, imminent danger. Both his uncle and friend survived the attempted murder attack, but the "hit" on the teenage boy's life was still active. I drove him to the undisclosed location, the next day, where he lived for five months. I mentored him every two days, putting into place the "Safety-Future-Happiness" Solution Plan. I used all my East Side Heroes' mentoring techniques, I took him shopping for new non-gang style attire, I introduced him to the rest of my East Side Heroes' Family.

After six months, this fifteen year old boy, was a new man. He told me he didn't want to return to school, because it was too dangerous, in his case, it was true. So, he instead focused his energy working a full time job, six days a week.

He would often confide in me, with the concern, stating his concern, "My sister is still wearing a lot of gang colors."

A year later, his mom announced to the family that they were all moving to the same city where her son had successfully started a new life. So, because this young fifteen year old boy, dared to trust his mentor's guidance, his mom decided to break through the thick wall of despair that surrounds that city.

Now when this mom sees me, she says, *"Gracias por ayudarle a m'ijo."*

Her sad eyes tell me she still feels ashamed believing she has failed to keep her family safe. My eyes in return, smile as I explain, "You allowed your baby boy to leave home with a stranger on faith. He became the brave pioneer. And YOU changed the fate of your entire family's future - by doing what so many others have failed to do - believe in, trust in, and follow the "voice in the desert," who pleads every day "Change your way!"

"It's NOT what values you stand for, but WHO you stand WITH that counts." —Fr. G-Dog

-

RUNNING ON EMPTY

Zzzzzzz. Zzzzzz. cell phone rings. Time, 2,00am.
"Hello?"
"Hey *m'ija*, what going on?"
"Where you at right now?"
"k, I'll be there in twenty minutes."

I'd immediately start putting on my pants and shoes, trying to be quiet, but I slept in my parent's little apartment, where their bedroom was three steps away. My mom would always hear me and walk into the living room whispering.

"*Todo bien m'ijo?.*"

And I'd respond, "*Ahorita vengo, tengo que dar consejería.*"

I knew I wasn't getting paid to respond to crisis calls 24-7. But I was incapable of saying "no" when ever I'd hear mentees crying, asking for my help. As I grabbed my car keys, I would tell my mom, "*Regreso pronto.*"

My mom knew I had a calling in my life.

From 10 am to 10 pm, seven days a week, my cell phone would ring every thirty minutes every single day. I would also get about thirty emails per day from mentees other people, such as, parents, teachers, and other professionals. I would get a 2 a.m. crisis-call maybe once every two months. On average, I mentored 3-5 at-risk teens, in person, each day including Saturdays and Sundays. I would schedule my last mentoring appointment at 11 p.m., as I went from one intervention session to another. I never took a "weekend" off.

But, I was heading for self-destruction. Why? Because I was neglecting my health. They say, **"Once growth stops, decay starts."** As a human being, we have four parts to our holistic health, Mind, Body, Emotions, and Soul. I was neglecting my Body - by not eating enough, not sleeping enough, not resting enough, not exercising enough. I was neglecting my Emotions—by not venting my feelings to anybody, not working with a therapist, not allowing anybody to become a close friend, and self-sabotage any romantic relationships. I was neglecting my Mind—by neglecting my college studies never letting my mind rest, always trying to "fix" and accomplish something on my never ending to-do list. Lastly, I was neglecting my soul by staying focused on my flaws and errors and staying stuck in self-punishment, guilt, shame; instead of accepting forgiveness and peace.

As a result, I started getting two-week long severe flu's. Each flu started with the first day feeling super exhausted with no energy at all. The second day, a fever and a soar-throat that lasted 2-3 days, then a runny nose and heavy sneezing that hurt my entire body with aches for another three days. Then I would have a cough that would last an additional five days that would eventually cause me to lose my voice.

During these two long weeks of severe flu symptoms, I would never miss a day from work. Even if I had an "inspirational talk" scheduled at a high school, I would strain my voice to "talk" for one hour until I had no voice, forcing the words out—sounding like a thirteen year old boy going through puberty. In the year 2005, my body was screaming for rest, but I refused to rest. I would get a hard-core two week-long flu, then one week with no flu symptoms, then the flu would start again for another two weeks. This literal sick cycle repeated itself every three weeks, for the entire year of 2005, to the point where I counted fifteen of these two-week flus. And that still didn't stop me. I didn't take a single day of work for four years straight, even if I had no voice or suffering with a fever.

One night, I got out of a college class at 9 pm, I went straight to my office at Bellarmine to "work on stuff and check emails." I looked at the clock and it was 12 am midnight. Of course, I was still not done with my long to-do list, and I finally realized "I can be here all night and STILL not be done; because, I can always find something more to 'work on'." So I told myself, "I'll never be done, ..." but without guilt, I said "...but I'm done for tonight." So, I started permitting myself to "clock out" when I felt I had been productive enough throughout the day.

This decision permitted me to slow down. So, when I met My girlfriend, I was not in my regular hurry-mode. Three months prior, I would have cut the "meeting" short to about 30-40 minutes max. But since I was now trying to "live in the moment," my future-wifey and I sat, talked, and had dinner eating pizza for at least 2 hours. I believe things happen for a reason and set you up to be ready for the next stage. So, after five long years of being single, I finally chose to go out on "regular dates" and invest my time and energy in developing a deeper friendship with a woman, My girlfriend.

But as any weight lifter knows—your muscles don't feel sore until you stop lifting. Well, the same thing happened with me. Once I started to slow down my "sprinting" life style, I started experiencing withdrawal symptoms. These symptoms were brand new symptoms I had never experienced before because I had never actually stopped working before. New symptoms emerged every couple weeks. For instance, I felt exhausted and sleepy 24-7; I became very emotionally sensitive because of all the years I spent not allowing myself to feel MY feelings.

But the new symptoms kept coming. In addition to my fifteen severetwo-week long flu's a year; in addition to feeling exhausted and sleepy no matter how many hours I slept. In addition to feeling a shortness of breath due to my anxiety, in addition to not being able to shut off my "random racing thoughts" each night; in addition to having severe back aches in the mornings, none of these really concerned me. The only symptom that concerned me was when I was sitting at home, and I experienced a dizziness-movement that went from side to side for about three seconds. Not a regular spinning dizziness, but a light-headed dizziness like my equilibrium was off. At first, I dismissed it, guessing that maybe I got up too fast. But then that "light headed dizzy motion" happened again two months later, then again one month later, then again two weeks later, then again every three days. To the point where I would experience this "light headed, off balance, dizzy motion" ALL the time, regardless if I was sitting or walking or driving or just laying down. The only time it would stop, is when I laid down in bed and kept my eyes fixed on one single point on the ceiling or wall. If I moved my eyes from one object to another object, it would happen again. I had to quit my full time job at the Bill Wilson Center, falling behind on my bills because my health problems had me too worried and I wasn't able to concentrate at work.

I thought maybe it was my eyes? Maybe it was my ear drums? Maybe it was a tumor in my brain? So I made an appointment to see a doctor. When I arrived at the hospital, I asked the doctor to do blood work on me and insisted that they also do a "CAT Scan" of my brain. I put the results in My Mentor's hands as I lay on the white plastic board, as my head entered the inside of the circular machine and span around and around, taking an x-ray of my brain.

A couple of weeks later, I returned to the hospital to get my results. I was shocked and confused at what I heard from the doctor. The doctor said that my CAT-Scan results were "normal." I stayed quiet—perplexed. Finally, I asked the doctor, "So why am I getting these dizzy spells?," the doctor looked at me nonchalantly and said, "It's sounds like stress symptoms." I remember thinking, "This is B.S.," because I KNEW I wasn't stressed! How can it be stress? - I quit my full time job, I was now working only part time and charging my credit cards more often, I wasn't mentoring that much anymore, I wasn't doing any inspirational talks in schools anymore? Unsatisfied with that answer, I made another appointment with another doctor to get a second opinion. I met with the second doctor. This time I made a list of all the symptoms my body and mind had experienced the past year and I added a recent one—painful stomach aches. The doctor said he would run tests because it sounded like an ulcer. Again I waited for the results.

When I returned to the hospital two weeks later, this second doctor asked me one question, "How full is your plate? Your symptoms seem stress-related."

I responded, "Actually, my plate is empty. I'm doing less now than ever before."

But the doctor responded with what everybody else has said to me, "Slow down. Take some time for your self and relax."

Again I was annoyed, because i had slowed down. If I slowed down anymore I'd be unemployed! What came to my mind was a friend of mine who told me he had to take a year off because he had gotten "sick" from working too much. I didn't want that to happen to me. I refused to believe that I was "burning out." So, I went to talk to a third doctor and described all my symptoms. When this third doctor told me flat out and without hesitation, "Sounds like classic stress symptoms" I stopped fighting it and I finally was convinced. I stopped being in denial and trusted that my symptoms were stress-related.

Now surrendering, I asked the doctor, "So what do I do? What's the treatment plan?"

The doctor said the very same thing I heard from many other caring people had said, "You need balance."

So, from that day on, in early January 2006. I stopped mentoring, I stopped trying to be "all things for all people." I had burnt out.

"Pick battles big enough to matter, but small enough to win"—Jonathan Kozol

CHAPTER VI

TRANSFORMATION

While at the Capitol Drive-In with my new girlfriend, I caught a glimpse of a quote during the classic movie, "Fools Rush In." The quote spoke to me directly. The quote asked,

"What if you met the love of your life, but you found that you had to leave the life you love?"

Wow, deep. That quote stayed in my head, day after day, repeating to myself the same question—"What if you met the love of your life, but you found that you had to give up the life you love?" - Challenging myself to decide. I loved the life that I had built. It was convenient; it was safe; it was meaningful. Although I loved it, my lifestyle was also depleting my soul's energy, depleting my mind's sanity, depleting my body's health. I was at a cross roads dilemma. I either continue on the same path I created that served so many; or, I could take a risk and invest my time and energy into my friendship with her? I didn't know how I would feel about her in a year; but, what I did know was that this new friendship felt "right."

At first, I tried to live on both sides of the fence, trying to do it all. But that didn't work because trying to be boyfriend and workaholic resulted in my girlfriend sitting in my office for 3 hours watching me work and type. Or it meant ignoring phone calls from mentees due to dinner dates or weekend trips with my girlfriend. I failed to juggle both these lifestyles successfully. I had to decide. After much discernment, I decided to take a huge leap of faith. I decided to put an end to my previous lifestyle, and become open to a new era in my life, full of unknowns.

Sadly, my decision to take "time off" and "slow down" gave birth to another problem. I was diagnosed with General Anxiety Disorder in December of 2007. General Anxiety Disorder means that my mind will image the worst case scenario with anything and everything possible situation.

"The Best Way to Predict the Future, is to Invent it." — *Alan Kay*

I finally accepted one truth that ultimately set me free — without my health, nothing else matters. I committed myself without guilt to restoring my health. I put all my mentees lives in the hands of My Mentor, for Him to look after while I got well. I called my therapist Dr. Harold Hoyle and began healing one Wednesday at a time.

Like eagles, I had to make a life-saving decision. As the eagle reaches 50 years old, the eagle begins to realize that now its feathers have become too heavy to fly. The eagle looks down at its claws/talons and realizes that they too have become too long to catch its prey. If by some miracle the eagle can catch an animal, the eagle will soon realize that its beak has become too curved to successfully eat.

The eagle realizes that they will soon starve to death. Eagles must make a life or death decision. Either, 1. The eagle will say, "I'm not going to change for nobody! I was born with this body, so either you take it or leave it. It is what it is. If I change, none of my friends will recognize me. What you see is what you get." If the eagle stubbornly refuses to make any change—it will certainly die of starvation, unable to hunt.

All eagles know they were born with the free-will option to, 2. Go through the painful process of rebirth, such as a butterfly does within a cocoon as well as snakes do when they shed their previous skin. This eagle's process of rebirth begins with the eagle choosing to forcefully pluck out all of their heavy feathers using their long talons. The eagle then chooses to pull off its long talons using its curved beak. Finally, the eagle chooses to slam his beak against a hard rock until it breaks it off completely. Then the injured eagle sits. This injured eagle sits in pain, high up on a mountain top, and waits. These eagles will wait until everything grows back anew, reborn, able to hunt and live for 30 more strong years!

"If you want something you've never had, you have do things you've never done!"—Thomas Jefferson

So, I did something I'd never done before. I started saying "no." My girlfriend saved my life. Meeting My girlfriend help me see beyond 30 years old. For the 1st time in my life I began to ask myself, "What do I want to do on a Saturday?" Instead of asking myself, "Who needs my care and attention most this Saturday?"

"The best way to find love—is to give love;
The fastest way to lose love—is to hold on too tight;
The only way to grow in love—is to give that person wings."

"There is only misfortune in not being loved. But there is misery in refusing to love." —Rod McKuen

"Si - el grano - de trigo no muere—si no muere—solo quedará.
Pero - si muere—en abundancia dará—un fruto eterno—que nunca morirá." —John 12,24

WARRIOR? OR SAVAGE?

Gazing out the window of "El Camion," I couldn't believe I was staring at an actual jungle! I finally realized why people always carry machetes in a jungle. Because its impossible to walk into the jungle. Every step you take, there are twisted looking tree limbs and vines crisscrossing in every path and direction. These jungles stretched out for miles and miles all over the land. As a day-dreamer, I of course began to imagine about all of the "What if's..." worst case scenarios.

I began thinking to myself, "what if... there was a huge Tsunami wave right now, right here? All that ocean water would wash people deep into the jungle or, the ocean water would carry all the jungle's snakes and spiders to the people! IF that happened, what would I do??" Day dreaming is how I entertain myself, that's why I'm never bored. It's like I constantly play these detailed movies and stories in my head, nonstop.

As my wife and I neared our destination, I look out the bus window and see dozens of super shacks and tiny houses everywhere. What's more fascinating is that actual Mayan descendants still live here in these isolated communities. What surprised me, however, was that even in these very remote villages, I still noticed "Coca-Cola" posters marketing their product.

Three hours later, we finally arrived at our destination. Our tour guide led the way, as we entered the iron gates. As we walked onto a large grassy clearing, I saw it....From a distance, through the top of the trees, I was in awe at what I was seeing....I was in silent disbelief, at the fact that I was HERE; but, at the same time, I was so happy that I was sharing this magical moment with my divine soul mate.

We walked, hand-in-hand, then we stood there, holding hands, speechless. Uttering the only word "Wow," which said it all. My girlfriend and I were standing on holy ground - in the physical presence of one of the official "Seven Wonders of the World", "CHI-CHEN-ITZA" Pronounced, "Chee-Chen-Eat-SAH". Chi-Chen- Itzá is a massive pyramid, made of pure stone, called, "Kukulkan" also known as "El Castillo". My wife and I decided to ditch our tour group and experience the ancient Mayan community our way, and at our pace. My top 4 favorite structures that we saw, were, "El Castillo," "The Temple of Warriors," "El Caracol" Observatory, and "the Ball Court." There were hundreds of Mayan people present there - selling their arts and crafts, jewelry, paintings, and pottery. As we walked through this ancient site, I observed several indigenous elders carving wooden canes and masks, with their small pocket knives. My wifey and I bought the most artifacts out of all the visitors/tourists we were carrying at least six bags of full of stuff.

Suddenly, a short, dark-skinned Mayan man, walked up to us carrying a beautiful and colorful pottery item in each hand. We declined to buy the pottery, but he freely offered to teach us a few words in legitimate Mayan language. As we stood there, fascinated by everything surrounding us, this young

Mayan shared with us the history and facts about the Mayan structures. He explained that the Maya held a market place next to "The Temple of Warriors," to buy, sell, and exchange food items and animals in the section called, "The Thousand Columns." He explained that the City of Chi-Chen-Itza was a lively place where all gathered to share in community and participate in the ancient ball game symbolic of the universe.

Our dark-skinned friend explained that the Mayan people were very advanced in mathematics and astronomy. "El Caracol" served as an observatory where Mayan astronomers made accurate measurements of the planet Venus. "The Pyramid of Kukulkan" is a physical calendar, because if you add up all of the steps leading up the pyramid, they total an accurate 365 steps.

Our new Mayan friend explained that the Mayan people were not blood thirsty savages as the movie, "Apocalypto" portrayed; but, instead, as this real life Mayan without a movie director directing him explained that the Mayans believed the Sun as the source of all life on earth, had to pass through earth beneath us. So, the Maya believed that the Sun needed actual human blood, to give the Sun strength to reemerge again and again every sun rise and give life to us all for one more day. The fact is, the Maya People never took life for granted. So, it was considered the greatest honor for a person to sacrifice his or her life at "The Temple of the Warriors," so that the rest of his or her people on earth could continue living.

According to Mayan astrology, my Mayan Zodiac birth- sign is "Xul" the Baby Jaguar. I was born under the

Venus Evening Star, which states, *"The world knows them for their big ideas, but to their family they are loved and feared for their big emotions."* I was so impressed, inspired, and empowered by the Mayan history, that when I got home, I researched other ancient cultures. What I learned was that all around the earth, existed Ancient Warriors. From the Samurai Warriors of Japan, the Celtic Warriors of Europe, the Masais Warriors of Africa, the Vikings from Scandinavia, the Aztec Warriors of Mexico, the Mayan Warriors of Central America—ALL of these Warriors believed in honor and decency. These true Warriors were always on constant alert to protect their home, women, children, and the elders. These honorable Warriors protected their family against unprovoked attacks of the savages.

Warriors believed in **"Preserving Life, Not Destroying Life."** —Nirmalya

Savages believe in the opposite. Savages believe in committing crimes of murder, rape, and theft to gain control, power, and spread terror and fear. Warriors believe in defense not offense. Warriors do not seek revenge. Warriors do not believe in going out to attack and ravage another's village; but instead, Warriors choose to remain in peace with all their neighbors to continue sharing goods. Given these two role model types, I choose to live as a Warrior for Peace, who protects without the desire to dominate nor intimidate.

"It's your Attitude, not your Aptitude, that will determine your Altitude in life." —Zig Ziglar

WARRIOR OF LIGHT

It was a hot summer day; my friend and I were driving to the gym again. We had our windows rolled up to feel the cool air conditioning from the A/C. As we were driving and talking, I saw a distraught seventeen-year old girl, from the right side of my peripheral vision, walking towards traffic! I noticed the tears and fear in her eyes, unsure if she should risk crossing the busy street.

I asked myself silently, "Why was she in a hurry?" Two seconds later, I understood why. Her much bigger boyfriend was closing in behind her. Honestly, my first thought was, "This is none of my business, just a young couple having some 'relationship drama'." So, I ignored it and kept driving to my destination.

But, as I drove away, my Warrior Spirit within me protested. My inner spirit disagreed and objected to my human logic. My "Agape Love" dictates that I can NOT neglect this young woman in distress. As this moral dilemma battled within me, my friend said four words that settled my internal dispute, "Did you see that?" When I heard the concerned tone in his voice, I knew the right decision had to be made. I immediately made a left U-turn.

When we "rolled up on him," I thought the woman-beater would automatically stop, since "witnesses" had arrived. I assumed decency and common sense would enter into his conscience, but I assumed wrong. Instead, this bully of women directed his rage towards my car. He put his hands up yelling, "Mind your own fucken business!" Then, as he walked towards us, he reached his right hand behind his back to his waist band. My brain froze and my breathing stopped for about 3 seconds with an "Ohhh SHIT" reaction, because we both thought he was pulling out a gun! This guy, instead pulled out a knife and walked over to my side of the car window He had the knife in his right hand and was yelling at me "Get out of the car! Come on! Get out of the fucken car!"

    At that moment I had to decide what to do? Do I try to talk to him, until he cools down?; Or do I speed off and keep my friend and I safe, forgetting about this young girl's wellbeing? Or do I pull out my knife and get out of the car and see who's quicker to puncture the heart? I decided too choose option "A," as I transformed myself into a freaking "hostage negotiator." My friend was on his cell phone with the police at this time as well.

    The Domestic Violence Offender walked back to where his girlfriend was, and he began slapping her in the face more. I immediately placed my vehicle in reverse and drove back to where he was to get his attention away from his victim, which worked! - Because he started coming towards my vehicle again. But, then he returns his attention to his girlfriend and slaps her in the face again. Next thing that happens is a police car rolls up, the officer jumps out of his car, pulls his gun out, points it at the boyfriend still holding the knife in his hand, and placed him under arrest.

When I asked my friends about my decisions, I got many different opinions. But, by far, the best response I received was, "Hey, nobody got hurt, and that girl now has a chance to get away from that abusive relationship by seeking help. You might have saved her life today?

"If you don't appreciate it, you don't deserve it." — Terry Josephson

"One man's garbage is another man's treasure." — Yotam Ottolenghi

I know I took the risk of getting involved in this "None of my business" situation. But I do not regret my decisions, because I asked myself, "What would my Aztec and Mayan ancestor Warriors have done? Would any true Warriors from any other culture choose to ignore this teenage female getting physically abused?" I'm proud to know that their brave spirit is still flows inside my Mestizo veins. I hope My Mentor continues to guide me and put me at the right place and the right time to help others who are in need, regardless of the risk. Because Savages despise and hate Warriors; Savages love the Darkness of Evil.

We will ALL face our last day, but I'd rather go to the next life knowing that I served, followed, and obeyed the right boss with divine orders. This hot summer day, My Mentor reminded me I am now part of the "Family Business," thus, this teenage girl WAS worth my time and life, as part of my

Mentor's Tribe. My Warrior Spirit makes it VERY clear to me that my business is NOT "to mind my busy-ness," but instead, reminds me that my mission and purpose on this earth is to protect, heal, and inspire.

For, *"If we have no peace, it is because we have forgotten that we belong to each other."* -Mother Teresa

"People are often hurtful and selfish;
Forgive them anyway.
If you are kind, people may accuse you of selfish, ulterior motives;
Be kind anyway.
If you are successful, you will win some false friends and some true enemies;
Succeed anyway.
If you are honest and sincere, people may cheat you;
Be honest and sincere anyway.
What you spend years building, someone could destroy overnight;
Build anyway.
If you find serenity and happiness, people will be jealous;
Be happy anyway.
The good you do today, people will often forget tomorrow;
Do good anyway.
Give the world the best you have, and it may never be enough;

Give the world the best you've got anyway.
You see, in the final analysis, it is between you and your God;
It was never between you and them anyway. - Mother Teresa

CHAPTER VII

DEJA-VU

I was standing outside, on the side walk, just feeling the stillness of the streets at that rare moment. As I stood there, breathing in the calm air, I see a familiar face crossing the street. Our older homeboy "from across the street" had a huge smile on his face, as he pushed a baby-stroller across the street towards me.

"Hey, check out my baby boy!," He said proudly as a new papa.

The older homie "from across the street" then said, "Look, this stroller has big wheels—so we can chase Sureños! Ha-ha!"

As we took a stroll with the stroller, around the block towards another homie's house, a white car slowly drove past us in the opposite direction. The car slowed down enough for another Norteño in the passenger side to stick his head out the window and calmly challenge us with his chin-up, hand-gesture, and statement.

"Wutz'up?"

We knew how to read the body language of a threat; we knew how to read "the look," we knew how to read the calm before the storm.

My older homie, handed me the handles of the stroller with his baby boy, and began jogging behind the white car.

The Norteño dude was still hanging his chest and head out the window perplexed at why our older homie was calmly jogging at a casual pace towards them? This was another day in the hood. The dude in the car activated our older homie's "automatic response." My older homie wasn't mad, he was just in "handling business mode."

As my older homie got closer to the car, I saw my older homie reach with his right hand to his right back pocket, grab his pocket knife, and swing to stab the Norteño threw the passenger window. "SSKUURRRR"—the car driver quickly pulled on the steering wheel to save his friend from getting stuck in the neck or chest.

When I heard the tires screech loudly, my automatic response was activated, because every time I heard tires screech, I knew that was a car making a U-turn to try to run me over, so I grabbed on the handle bars of the baby stroller and pushed and sprinted half a block to another homie's house to get the baby boy to safety.

I was thirteen years old on this particular day. Our older homie was seventeen. A few seconds later, I saw my older homie, calmly walking around the corner towards me - again, strolling nonchalantly. We went back to the front of my apartments to hang out. We knew what was coming. We knew in about forty-five minutes, the car would return with more heads.

We waited. Because *"If you don't learn from the past, you're doomed to repeat it."—Winston Churchill*

Our older homie "from across the street" went to prison

for about ten years, after shooting someone with a shotgun. He's been out now for about six years. His baby boy, is now a seventeen year old teenager. His baby boy, whom I took to safety the firts day I meet him, is now an "active" gang member, and his dad is a proud papa. Both hang out in front of the same house, and wait for rival gang members to come back for round two, round three, round four, round five.

Because, *"If we don't learn from the past, we are doomed to repeat it."* — **Winston Churchill**

I wish I could save them both. But I can't help those who don't want to get out. So, I'm offering a helping hand to those who want a different life. A life on the "outs."

And I'm giving the same plea that Cesar Chavez gave, when he told the people, *"Sal Si Puedes!"* — **Cesar Chavez**

"Our greatest fear is not that we are inadequate. Our deepest fear is that we are powerful beyond measure. It is our light, not our darkness that most frightens us. We ask ourselves, 'who am I to be brilliant, gorgeous, talented, fabulous?' Actually, who are you NOT to be? You are a child of God. Your playing small does not serve the world. Nothing is enlightening about shrinking so that other people won't feel insecure around you. We were born to make manifest the glory of God that is within us. It is not just in some of us; it is in everyone. As we let our light shine, we unconsciously permit other people to do the same. As we are liberated from our fear, our presence automatically liberates others." —Marianne Williamson

"If you have enemies - good. That means you stood up for somebody in your life." — Winston Churchill

"Every night that I fall asleep I die. And every morning that I awake, I am reborn again." — Gandhi

"Just when the caterpillar thought the world had ended — it became a butterfly" — Barbara Haines

"Leaders Create Leaders, Not Followers" — Tom Peters

CPSIA information can be obtained
at www.ICGtesting.com
Printed in the USA
BVHW091812090323
660111BV00001B/18